write
what
you
mean

write what you mean

Allen Weiss

A HANDBOOK OF BUSINESS COMMUNICATION

amacom

A DIVISION OF AMERICAN MANAGEMENT ASSOCIATIONS

Library of Congress Cataloging in Publication Data
Weiss, Allen.
  Write what you mean.

  Includes index.
  1. Communication in management—Handbooks, manuals,
etc. I. Title.
HF5718.W42   658.4'5   77-11956
ISBN 0-8144-5453-4

First Printing

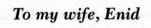

To my wife, Enid

preface

The business writer has one primary purpose: to get a message across to the right people. Everything that is said about business writing must be directed toward that purpose.

The advice *Write for the audience!* is useful in its place, just as the cheerleaders' plea *Hold that line!* may bolster a team's morale; but in the end the coach who shows his players how to block, pass, run, and tackle contributes more directly to his team's victories than all the cheering sections at all the games.

Similarly, it is more useful to explain the practical techniques of business writing than to repeat the admonition to write clearly. Accordingly, this book will develop a rationale for business writers to follow—and along the way, myths will be exploded and empty slogans exposed.

Intended primarily for people in business, government, and other organizations, this book seeks to promote understanding in the communication of ideas, to make life easier for those who write or speak, and to lighten the burden of those who are exposed repeatedly to memoranda, reports, and speeches. Since thinking is mainly verbal, facility of expression is also helpful to ordinary thought processes: good writers think clearly, because careful writing and clear thinking support each other.

As a creative activity, writing can be gratifying to people who work at mastering the basic techniques. Perhaps more to the point, they will be amply rewarded. Articulate people sell their talents more effectively, and therefore progress more rapidly in organizational settings.

All of which is another way of saying, "You, too, can write for fun and profit." You really can. The skills of business writing and speaking can be learned; they can be enjoyed; and they can be used to promote your career.

ALLEN WEISS

contents

I | getting ready

1 | *through the eyes of the beholder*

Business is transacted by people writing or speaking to one another. Organizations depend on communicators to keep things going. Hence, the business writer's first objective is to convey messages. Self-expression is secondary, self-indulgence is embarrassing, and self-amusement is wasteful. The medium is not the message in business; substance and readability are more important. The transmission of *real* messages to *real* people is what business writing is all about; and it relies on *audience direction* for its results.

It takes two sides to communicate: a writer needs readers and a speaker must have listeners. Audience direction is the method by which writers and speakers persuade persons on the receiving end to stay with the subject; the method focuses on audience attitudes and levels of knowledge.

An analogy to audience direction can be found in business operations: the modern corporation conducts its affairs according to a methodology that is *market-oriented*. Before a manufacturer commits resources to producing large quantities of an item, its potential sales are forecast from collected data relating to market demand. As a corollary, new products are planned with the wants and needs of consumers in mind. Packaging is also made attractive to prospective buyers; and this orientation to consumers is further reflected in the methods of salespersons who gauge their prospects' interests and susceptibilities, so that each sales pitch may be slanted more effectively. In every case, the orientation is to the persons on the receiving end.

When this selfishly inspired concern for the other person's views eventually determines one's own actions through a process of continuous response to feedback, the situation resembles the other-directed behavior that David Riesman described in his perceptive analysis of our competitive-enterprise (business-oriented) society and that he differentiated from tradition-directed and inner-directed behavior. This book, however, is not the place to consider arguments over the effects of competition on personality. It is accepted that manufacturers should gear their production to consumer wants and needs. Likewise, *business persons should write with their readers' wants and needs in mind.* That is the first rule of business writing.

In a sense, the letters and reports of people doing business advertise their views and their expertise. Like advertising, therefore, business writing should reach out for the attention of its readers and strive to hold their interest while conveying a message. Also, in the best examples of business communication, every last detail must ring true. Nothing destroys reader confidence as surely as misstatements of fact, slipshod thinking, or exaggerated claims. Accordingly, *major concomitants of audience direction are accuracy and moderation.*

Who reads memos and letters?

For every piece of business writing, there must be a set of readers; different sets of readers can be expected to hold different attitudes and raise different questions. Indeed, the same individual may react one way to memoranda, another to letters, and still another to reports.

Ed Johnson likes to have his mail sorted so that he can read the intracompany memoranda first. Scanning each memorandum, he asks a series of questions: What are the writer's real and ostensible motives? Does the memo seek to inform, persuade, encourage, or involve the addressees? Are there any hidden messages? Ed proceeds to analyze each memorandum carefully, probing always for indications of the writer's true intent.

Just such careful scrutiny of her memos is the first point for Polly Richardson to bear in mind whenever she sets out to write one. Relieved of all obligation to go out of her way to attract the reader's attention or hold his interest, Polly must accept instead the certainty that her motives will be questioned. A slip on her part will be sure to raise doubts as to her credibility.

Ed Johnson, after reading the internal memos on his desk, turns next to letters from outside the company. Those letters that continue previous correspondence are expected to be responsive to the earlier exchanges. Indeed, Ed's first judgment of all such letters is based on their responsiveness. Letters that break new ground naturally raise fresh questions: What's that about? Should it be addressed to me or to someone else? What should I do about it? Many letters, including promotional mail, evoke a shrug of indifference while being consigned to a wastebasket. Ed doesn't have time to waste on these letters, unless they're likely to generate ideas, or help Ed's personal program of continuing, if haphazard, education.

Promotional mail

Despite the jokes on the subject, it would be wrong to say that all the promotional mail Ed receives is categorized as junk mail and automatically discarded. On the contrary, he frequently studies the course outlines that come to him unsolicited. A number of organizations send these outlines, and Ed derives several kinds of information from them:

◇ An overview of a subject he is only vaguely familiar with. Ed feels that his perusal of course announcements has given him a virtual grasp of the scope of many subjects.

◇ A logical arrangement of the topics included in the subject matter of a course. As subjects broaden to comprise new areas, Ed believes he can sometimes discern incipient trends by remaining alert to changes in course announcements.

◇ A glossary of the buzz words that are bandied about. Jargon has a way of shucking off some words while adopting others, and an occasional review helps Ed to feign knowledgeability in some situations.

It may seem that Ed's careful inspection of course announcements serves no loftier purpose than to provide him with a superficial familiarity with the newsy aspects of a variety of subjects. However, when he contemplates the snow jobs he has pulled off, the easy victories he has won over jargoneers no more profound than himself, and the delays he has wangled by sounding immediately knowledgeable, Ed is satisfied that his reading time has been well spent. He will go on reading letters that carry scraps of useful information. Accordingly, those business writers who hope to capture Ed's attention through letters should remember to offer him the kinds of information he looks for.

Ed is convinced that his own efforts at communicating are facilitated by his keeping in touch with the latest in business fashions. Hence, writing that projects a modish appearance is more likely to evoke an interested response from Ed—and many others like him. They are guided by a pragmatic concept: If there is a chance to learn something flashy from a piece of mail—a new idea, a fresh juxtaposition of old ideas, a possibly useful buzz word—they read on. But completely empty phrases and hackneyed expressions, no matter how glibly presented, quickly wear thin and just as quickly turn these readers off.

Readers of reports

While a business writer like Polly Richardson must accommodate her thinking to the Ed Johnsons, she must also write for her boss. He sees all letters before they go out, and he generally tries to justify his position and salary by making suggestions, criticizing here and there, voicing objections, or being "helpful" in other revealing ways. For her own good, Polly has to keep her boss in mind. In no case, however, should she—or any other business writer— abandon the pursuit of excellence on the specious grounds that whatever is written will be revised anyhow, or worse still, that, judging by the quality of his own writing, the boss seems to prefer a heavy style and substandard English.

A report is likely to go to the business writer's boss, that boss's boss, and others at higher levels. Each boss up the line will wonder, "How can I look good for having released this document?" and he will feel justified in tampering to fulfill his need to bask in reflected glory. But others outside the line of authority on the organization chart will tend toward views that range from envious to disinterested to openly critical. Moreover, once a report has been released, it will probably circulate beyond the original distribution list; the readers of all but strictly technical reports are likely to be a mixed lot, owing not so much to their diverse backgrounds as to their divergent motives and attitudes—and their varying propensities for mischievous conduct. Sophisticated audience direction includes a healthy distrust of business readers and an acute awareness of defensive tactics.

Writing for publication

Daydreams aside, few people in business contemplate writing articles for publication. Yet Harry Burns has concluded that there is no more certain way to pursue recognition and acquire a reputation among colleagues in his field, to burst the limitations of a confining situation, to extend his influence beyond his employer's walls, and, at the same time, to enhance his prestige among immediate associates. Furthermore if any person in business or the professions has something to say and is willing to work at learning how to say it, then his interests will be served best by starting early to publish articles that will have a cumulative impact.

In submitting manuscripts, Harry has a choice of magazines, each with its own readership and each with an editor whose job it is to keep that readership reasonably content. These editors and readers have become the new audience for Harry to reach; the challenge for him is to answer each prospective reader's question, "Why should I bother with your article?" To be sure, in a heterogeneous audience Harry must expect to find many individuals who will not, and perhaps should not, read what he has written. But the challenge remains: to find a bloc of readers and hold their interest while he tells them something.

Audience characteristics

Despite their heterogeneity, business readers have a great deal in common. Since the audience-directed writer is concerned with essentials like accumulated knowledge, fundamental beliefs, basic motivation, and lasting attitudes, interests, and objectives—rather than with incidental traits, ephemeral moods, or unpredictable vagaries—the area of agreement is generally quite broad. For instance, it is ordinarily practical to generalize about the education, backgrounds, and preconceptions of an audience of accountants or social workers or personnel specialists; and a great many common interests and goals characterize such groups as drug salesmen, hospital administrators, or club managers.

By carefully analyzing the list of audience characteristics, a business writer must derive a sound hypothesis concerning the specific interests that can be expected and that should be exploited with regard to the readership of the report that is being prepared. Manifestly, even a limited knowledge of his audience enables Harry Burns to direct his writing to his readers to some extent; the more precise his evaluation of the *essential* characteristics of his audience, and the more closely he can relate a succession of themes to those interests, the more effective his audience-directed approach will be.

In addressing a memorandum to a handful of people she knows, Polly Richardson can evaluate her audience in fairly specific terms. Nevertheless, she is wise to avoid a narrow description of any audience, even a "known" one. Give readers credit for having interests beyond the narrow confines of their specialty. Treat them with respect. Don't underestimate their capacity, and don't talk down to them.

In particular, when Polly undertakes to persuade people to act in a certain manner, she must acknowledge her audience's selfish individual interests, and she must cope with prevalent fears that stand in the way of her objective. Self-interest and fear are the most important of the audience characteristics to be analyzed, especially for the business writer who hopes to wield some influence. For she can best pursue her own advantage by showing others how to pursue theirs, and by overcoming resistance born of fear. To put the matter another way, prospective benefits to readers must be perceived by them as being truly in their own interests, and not as threats to their security. And to comprehend an audience's perception, it is necessary to analyze some relevant characteristics.

Misconceptions about quality

A doubtful hypothesis that retards the development of good business writing is the statement one occasionally hears that it doesn't matter whether the writing is substandard as long as it is understood by the reader. The fallacy here is that a writer blandly assumes his readers will grasp his meaning even though no agreement exists as to the writing standards to be employed. For business writing, accepted grammar and standard English usage certainly offer the greatest assurance that reader and writer are riding the same vehicle. At any rate, whenever a misunderstanding develops—because either the writer ignored standard usage or the reader was poorly informed—let the fault lie with the other party. In writing or in reading, it is better to hold up one's own end. Don't assume that the other party is a slob—lest you lose your own reputation in the end.

Indeed, when the Ed Johnsons detect signs of substandard English, they will harbor uncertainties about a careless writer's real meaning. One of the questions Ed raises is, "Does this writer know how to say what he means?" This is followed by, "Does this writer appear to understand his subject? How good are his credentials? Can his judgment be relied on? Is there anything new in what he writes?" Good writing gets better marks among readers.

If muddled thinking and slovenly writing prompt uncertainty among readers, showiness arouses suspicion. A dense style, unfathomable and obscure, can succeed only in leading a frustrated Ed Johnson to throw up his hands and question both the writer's ability to put a message across and the actual presence of a message at all. Similarly, ostentation or pomposity can make a reader wonder whether the writer has confidence in his message. Surely straightforward logic can be expressed in direct terms. That is the essence of good business writing.

When an atypical, incompetent editor of an undistinguished publication remarked to a small group of business editors, "You can polish articles to the finest literary style, but our readers will never know the difference," this strange hypothesis was attacked on several grounds. One editor reported that reader surveys conducted by his magazine showed a distinct preference for well-written articles over poorly written ones of similar content, courageously published as a test. Other editors argued that, although a literary style is irrelevant to business writing, their readers' critical capabilities were varied and not to be lightly dismissed; that

the most discerning readers are precisely the ones a professional editor seeks to hold anyhow; and that it is always
necessary for professionals to put forth their best work in
any case.

Professional engineers or accountants, no less than professional writers, should express themselves to the best of
their ability; and professional editors carry added responsibility for maintaining standards of quality. Obviously, standard usage must not be flouted in manuscripts submitted to
professional editors; as in other fields, there may be duds
among business editors, but true professionals uphold high
standards of quality as a mark of respect for their readers
and their profession.

Centering on the readers

The audience-directed approach is an adequate guide to
gaining acceptance among readers. It should not be made
into a stumbling block for business writers to trip over.
Specifically, it would be silly for Polly Richardson to carry
her concern for audience reaction to the specific backgrounds of individual readers. That road leads to frustration.
Readers who are not stamped out of a single mold cannot be
catered to in every detail of their divergent viewpoints. It is
sufficient for Polly to direct messages at a generalized concept of a typical reader in the audience, concentrating on
essentials only. Having developed such a concept, she must
keep it constantly in mind.

Polly may of course want to watch her boss's mood before presenting him with a controversial draft she has prepared. But effectiveness in writing cannot be served by extensive research into what everyone in the company will
have for breakfast on the day a report is released. Nor should
any business writer allow herself to be troubled by
irrelevancies.

Instead of pursuing chimeras, Polly can rely on a
method of selecting a few representative figures and writing
for them. She won't miss essential readers by much. In addi-

tion, mastery of certain writing techniques will help her considerably. (Technique and style are dealt with more fully in later chapters.) For example, a suitable business style is literate, but not literary. Those who read extensively will recognize a writer's willingness to work at expressing thoughts properly for their benefit. Such an endeavor requires educated diction, which in turn demands of Polly a reasonably strong vocabulary. Also important is precision in selecting words. Grammatical correctness is another requirement, but purism is to be avoided. In fact, purist misconceptions about grammar must be discarded as an unnecessary burden to a business writer. Briefly, standard usage is the best single guide for the business writer who wants to be read and understood.

All the foregoing terms and concepts are explained in this book. In addition, advice is given on acquiring an easier writing style. The business world has moved from the starched cuffs of the beginning of this century to the shirt sleeves of the present. Whereas a few courageous women wearing the bustles of their day once had to overcome strong prejudices before they could so much as enter into the business world, their great granddaughters have now introduced slacks and miniskirts to the modern office. These echoes of profound social change suggest yet another precept: *It is only fitting that business writing discard the vestiges of a stuffy formalism*. Accordingly, this book is dedicated to easier communication and a sensible approach to business writing in accordance with the social customs of the day.

The writer's attitudes

Audience direction is central to good business writing; and an excellent basis for reaching out to readers is an attitude toward them that is friendly, courteous, and helpful. However, considerable effort must go into maintaining such an attitude; courtesy alone demands that the business writer exercise great care, that he review his work until all ambiguity has been removed, and that he rewrite his report until it is readable.

Audiences should of course never be scolded, talked down to, or antagonized. An attitude of friendliness will protect a business writer from these mistakes—and they are clearly mistakes, despite the frequency with which they are encountered. Also, a desire to be genuinely helpful will not permit a business writer to abuse his audience with self-preening, strutting, or posturing. Pedantry, pretentiousness, and arrogance show through—and always to bad effect. Turgidity and bombast are telltale signs of an improper attitude toward the reader.

The listening audience

The audiences a person speaks to in a business setting are likely to have many characteristics in common with the readers of his business writing. By and large, what has been said of readers will describe listeners as well. However, a few additional points must be borne in mind when one is preparing to face an audience of listeners.

A listener's attention will wander from time to time. When something similar happens to Ed Johnson, the business reader, he may go back and reread a passage, if the writer has succeeded in holding his interest up to that point. Not so with a listener. When her attention begins to stray, a clear danger exists that she will be lost permanently, unless the speaker resorts to frequent repetition and visual aids. The injunction, *Tell them what you're going to tell them; then tell it to them; then tell them what you've told them* is a sound prescription for speakers—although only occasionally so for writers. At transitional points between subjects, recapitulate what has just been said before introducing the next subject. Also, immediate repetition of words, phrases, or sentences helps them to sink in.

A reader can go back and reread a passage; he can stop and look up unfamiliar words; listeners cannot. Therefore, vocabularies for speaking should be more limited than vocabularies for writing. Be especially careful in the use of jargon. As a way of overcoming problems with unfamiliar words, it is useful to flash strange terms and their definitions on a screen, for reinforcement, or to write them on a board for continuing reference. Used in this manner, visual aids return to the speaker some of the advantages a writer enjoys.

Although listeners and readers share many characteristics, and although the primacy of audience direction still holds in both cases, the few differences between business speaking and business writing require that a manuscript for a speaker reflect a listener-oriented approach that deviates from strict reader orientation. In a word, the script for a speech is not an article meant to be scrutinized on a printed page; adjustments are needed to adapt either mode to the other.

1- Tell them what you're going to tell them
then, tell it to them
then, tell them what you've told them

2 | *basic options*

After a person has decided to send a message to a particular audience, his next step is to select a medium. So he asks: Will a telephone call suffice? Would a visit be appropriate? Should the matter be put in writing? Is a formal report called for? The admonition to put everything in writing is not a reliable guide. There are too many papers floating around now. A better procedure is to recognize certain selection criteria.

Several considerations should influence the choice of a suitable medium. First, the *purpose* of the message may be to persuade others to do things or do them a certain way, to explain accepted procedures, to win people over to a favored train of thought, to inform them of the status of things or of changes in a fluid situation, to answer questions that have arisen, to raise doubts in previously untroubled minds, to defend an action, to report on an investigation, or merely to leave a record of one's activities.

Frequently, the purposes of a message are mixed. Instructions will not suffer if they are given motivational content; on the contrary, it is a good idea to encourage people to follow the rules as they are spelled out. A report automatically informs the reader and provides a record; it may, at the same time, attempt persuasion. The pursuit of one purpose does not preclude the pursuit of others.

Nevertheless, the purposes of a message directly influence the selection of a medium. Persuasion is often better attempted orally; immediate reactions can then be observed and positions appropriately modified; similarly negotiation and compromise are all but inconceivable in written exchanges. On the other hand, when defensive tactics are called for, it is best to put everything in writing and to avoid being trapped by others into uttering careless statements. At the same time, in deciding to forgo the advantages conferred by the simple act of making a phone call and choosing instead the more involved process of setting words on paper, one leaves the recipient of a memo to infer defensive—perhaps even devious—motives. Consequently excessive memo writing should be shunned, but the written record itself—a limited number of meticulously worded memoranda—will generally serve as a good defensive weapon, because distortion and misrepresentation are precluded thereby.

Second, the need for *audience direction* affects the communicator's selection of a medium. The choice must take into account the relative potentials of all available media in reaching the audience and accomplishing the purpose. For example, to explain something to a number of people quickly requires either a memorandum or a hurriedly called meeting. Frequently, only the memorandum is practicable—even if a meeting could have been called, the insufficiency of the notice would most likely have caused resentment. On the other hand, if the opinions of a few people are needed immediately, a series of telephone calls may be the most effective method to use. Here again however, the caller must be careful not to arouse suspicion, for the urgent request for an unconsidered opinion is an overworked ploy of devious people. So the question becomes, In what different ways will the audience react to the urgency of a telephone request, to a memorandum asking for written replies, to the inconvenience of a call for a meeting, to the formality of a report? An auxiliary question is, Which medium will be most effective in achieving the primary purposes with the chosen audience?

Third, the twin trends toward *informality* and *time-saving methods* are also influencing the choice of business media. Whereas memoranda have been reserved for intra-company use and letters are generally sent to outsiders, a growing custom permits sending brief notes to close associates anywhere. Letters of transmittal are often reduced to a few words on the sender's business card or memo sheet. Actually, these media lend a personal touch that may be missing from more formal modes of communication.

Fourth, *organization size* counts in important ways. A supervisor can conduct on-the-jòb training sessions or deliver oral instructions to a new employee, but uniform methods at multiple locations can be achieved only with formal manuals of standard procedures. In addition, informal talks to small groups may be supplanted at lower cost by a formal presentation designed for one large group, convened perhaps for another purpose.

Sometimes the medium and the audience are chosen together. When writing for publication, Harry Burns wants to reach a specific audience and must therefore pick a magazine whose readers include that audience. In any case, on selecting a particular magazine, Harry determines the audience that will be available to receive his message. Within an organization, specific types of writing may be distributed automatically to predrafted lists: a memorandum on a given phase of operations will go to the people on one of these lists; a report on the same subject might go to a different set of people. Conceivably, a message may be structured as a report instead of as a memo: it is perhaps destined to reach a more influential audience, one that encompasses higher organizational levels.

Memoranda

Having concluded that immediate feedback from an on-the-spot exchange of thoughts is less important than going on record in a particular situation, Polly Richardson sets about writing a memo. At other times, she may follow up a conversation with a confirming memorandum, or answer a memo with a memo.

Always, she observes the rules of good memo writing. First, in keeping with the primary purpose of headings, the stated subject is made to correspond with a file category, so that filing and retrieval are facilitated. Second, the memo is structured so as to assist reader comprehension.

A business memo comes to the point quickly. The *why* of the message is stated at the outset; the *who* and *what* quickly follow; and the *where, when,* and *how* are appropriately dealt with before the end. *We need to improve our telephone service to customers, so we are making a few changes*—here is an opener that covers why and what. Audience direction requires that recipients know what to look for as they read on.

If a memo answers someone else's request for information or follows up something that was written previously, the opening should refer to the prior document in a brief statement of its subject and content. *You have asked how to handle certain problems created by the new law requiring such-and-such.* Or, *My previous memo of January 8 described a change in procedures for handling certain kinds of mail to outsiders. This memo elaborates on methods for sending mail to our own offices at other locations.*

Although it is wasteful to quote extensively from past correspondence, it is generally useful to summarize enough of what has transpired so that readers can follow what is being said without having to look back. A memo ought to stand on its own. However, since in many situations the record must be consulted—or will be by cautious readers—it may be an act of courtesy to attach a fresh copy of the old correspondence to the new document.

Above all, if Polly intends to ask the addressees to do something, she must be sure they know what it is she expects of them. A reader finds it exasperating to slog through dense verbiage and come up with no clear idea of its purpose. It is also self-defeating for the writer. Polly asks instead of ordering, and she is polite in wording a request. Nevertheless, she must make her meaning clear: if she wants something, she had better say so. It serves no purpose to make indirect passes by memo.

Letters

Much of what has been said about memoranda applies with equal force to letters. A telephone call may be quicker, cheaper, and more effective than a letter in many circumstances. Still, a confirming letter is often necessary; a letter of transmittal may accompany a report or other papers; and there will always be a place for other kinds of letters raising issues, clarifying situations, keeping in touch, notifying people of changes, asking for help, turning down requests, or sending condolences or congratulations.

More than other forms of writing, letters should carry a personal touch. Ordinarily, an expression of friendly concern is welcome to the recipient. Nothing is ever lost by opening and closing with little pleasantries. The busiest executive will not resent spending a few seconds to read words that indicate an appreciation of him or her as a person. Recall a recent meeting, or a pleasant association. Extend congratulations when appropriate. Remember that a holiday or weekend is coming up (surely you want your reader to enjoy it). Express gratitude for interest shown, help offered, advice given, or courtesies extended. A kind word will not be out of place.

Although entertainment for its own sake is seldom a legitimate purpose in business writing, all of us must surely welcome an occasional respite from the grimmer aspects of the world we live in. The typical organization offers most people little prospect of relief from routine; even the more fortunate employees suffer a larger share of uninteresting detail than they would like; so why not inject a humorous note here and there, a light touch to brighten the workday of a few of one's companions in business boredom, solemnity, and frustration?

In letters, as in memos, it is important not only to be human but also to come to the point quickly and directly. *It was good to hear from you again. I hope we can arrange to meet at the convention next month. Meanwhile, I'm taking certain actions in response to your suggestions. . . .* This is a much better opening than *Your letter of March 15 has been received. Please be advised that the contents are being studied. . . .*

As with memoranda, letters must be responsive to previous correspondence. The need is in fact greater when one is writing to persons outside the organization. With the advent of copying machines, a new type of quick response has developed: people now often note their replies directly on an initial letter received, make a photocopy of it, and send back that copy. Also, printers stock memorandum sets providing space for the sender's message on the left and the reply on the right; these sets are used in place of letters. In employing these methods, one must avoid the temptation to become too brief or too cryptic in one's reply. Polly can safely retain her prerogative to present the subject in her own way, without repeating what has already been said; she throws in a pleasantry or two, and if her message overflows to another sheet of paper, no harm has been done.

Other purposes are served by letters of transmittal. One that accompanies a report can summarize its highlights. Or the need for responsiveness may require that the letter say something about the commissioning of the study or the request for the report itself.

Minutes

For reasons that society may at long last be in the process of correcting, if a woman finds herself in a meeting with a committee of men, she is almost certain to be asked to act as secretary, which means that she will take minutes. Here, as elsewhere, women are automatically relegated to a role that carries the stigma of menial service. It's akin to bringing in the coffee. Nevertheless, even though the job is usually scorned, it can be made into a most important function.

Among its advantages, membership on a committee offers opportunities for meeting with others and enhancing one's standing among them. In writing up the minutes, Polly has a chance to demonstrate the skills she has taken the trouble to acquire. Her understanding of issues shows through in the way she presents conceptual material, and she has opportunities to paraphrase statements and improve on the original, selecting cogent remarks and summarizing lengthy discussions in a few pithy sentences. Thus given the opportunity to demonstrate her special skills, Polly makes her minutes a joy to read; and when they circulate to higher levels in the organization, she gains from the added visibility.

It pays to seize every opportunity to prepare the minutes of meetings, and it's wise to give the job one's best efforts, even at the cost of limiting one's participation in discussions. In preparing the minutes of a meeting, audience direction requires that you address several sets of readers: the members of the group have personal interests to protect, they want credit fairly distributed, and they are presumed to know the background of each discussion; nonmembers who receive the minutes are presumed to have an interest in the proceedings; future members may want to refer to the minutes for instruction or for definitive resolution of questions at issue.

Minutes constitute a recognized record of formal committee proceedings. By contrast, informal meetings seldom result in equivalent records. Yet these small meetings frequently end in agreements that need documentation. Whenever two or more people resolve to pursue a course of action in concert, they should have a written statement of their mutual understanding and their individual commitments. Analogous to the minutes of a formal meeting, such a confirming statement provides a reference for the parties to consult whenever disagreements crop up. It is a useful practice to prepare such a record and send it to the other parties immediately after a conference.

Neither formal minutes nor confirming letters should attempt to reconstruct a dialog as it occurred; they should rather present a synopsis of the discussion, including a fair and complete statement of each viewpoint. That is better than skipping back and forth simply because the original conversation was argumentative or because some speakers wandered into irrelevancies. Nor is repetition advisable merely because one speaker echoes what another said before him. Nonessentials must give way to clarity and accuracy. If there is any doubt as to a speaker's intentions, it is reasonable to phone him for confirmation of his views.

To summarize, the business of preparing minutes is sufficiently important to warrant special attention to the essentials of this specialized art. *The basic concern is with structure.* Discussions should be rearranged to bring out their substance with clarity and readability. Audience direction supersedes mere temporal exactitude.

Reports

Consultants, staff personnel, researchers, and operating personnel put out a variety of reports as the culmination of surveys, investigations, and projects. Frequently, all the effort that has gone into a study rides on the report and its acceptance. Yet people in business seldom allocate the time needed to write their reports adequately, and they are even less inclined to prepare themselves for what is surely one of the most important elements of a study. Reports are repeatedly thrown together under severe time pressures by people who have not prepared themselves for the undertaking—with predictably poor results.

Not only must every project's work plan allow time for

report writing, but the allotment of time should be worked out carefully to permit a product of the appropriate size and complexity. Sometimes a report is expected to be lengthy because the study itself is costly or important. Often a full report must be accompanied by an abbreviated version, which may or may not be incorporated into the early sections of the full report. In other companies it is customary to attach a précis to every report. Practices may differ between departments or locations of a single corporation. In general, audience direction will entail a full report for those who need one, a précis for the benefit of more casual readers, and a letter of transmittal that incorporates a synopsis.

In planning the issuance of a report, consideration should be given to format, tables, charts, and methods of reproduction. If a bibliography is to be included, it should be developed as the job proceeds. All these details are capable of emerging as troublesome obstacles—even crises—in the final hours of a project, unless adequate provision is made in advance to complete each aspect of the report properly and in an appropriate sequence.

Some commonly heard advice, however, is utterly impractical. Those who encourage others to write their reports in the course of conducting their studies should be made to swallow their own prescription. Actually, a report written piecemeal will have to be reworked and restructured: overall results will have to be superimposed, the relative importance of segments will have to be reassessed, and transitions between segments will have to be contrived. In the end, considerable time is likely to be lost from premature attempts to put words on paper; there can never be a saving in that method. Consultants who begin by attempting to write sections of their reports while conducting their engagements will end by blaming themselves or their associates for the inadequacy of their early efforts. They would do better to acknowledge the futility of a method that encourages premature writing exercises.

Manuals

A manual of procedures differs fundamentally from other types of writing in that readers are not expected to wade through a manual from cover to cover—except as a form of hazing sometimes inflicted on newcomers in initiation rites devised by sadistic older hands.

Manuals are intended for reference: to instruct employees in a new assignment, to resolve doubts, to coordinate activities, to standardize procedures at distant locations. In serving these purposes, an audience-directed manual must be unmistakably precise; it must guide readers in all sorts of foreseeable circumstances, explaining how to handle variations and exceptions. Such precision carries a price tag: no amount of editing or rewriting will ever make a procedure manual readable. In the trade-off between readability and precision, other kinds of writing can compromise at a half-way point, but not a manual. By its nature it is condemned to being unreadable forever—it's a waste of time to try to remake a ponderous pachyderm into a sleek feline.

The recipe style is helpful in writing procedures: *Staple the papers together in the following order . . .* is preferable to *The papers are then stapled together in the following order. . . .* A commonly used format for procedures has the appearance of a published play, with employees' titles appearing in place of performers' names and with specific chores replacing lines to be spoken. Another readers' aid is a set of flow charts that accompany written procedures and trace the movement of documents diagrammatically. Although these techniques all help to make procedures understandable, miracles cannot be expected. The stuff that manuals are made of is just not readable.

In-house publications

The discussion so far has covered such basic options for carrying a message as memoranda, letters, minutes, reports, and manuals. Each of these media has its special uses, advantages, disadvantages, and characteristics. Each should be chosen and designed to reach the right audience and to accomplish certain objectives.

Another communications medium used by many organizations is the house organ, variously appearing in the form of a magazine, a newsletter, or a bulletin. Although practices vary, in-house magazines are generally similar to other magazines and share with them a need for fresh material that will illuminate or augment the fund of knowledge. In-house newsletters report events and keep readers abreast of developments, often in a writing style with punch and a feeling for novelty. In-house bulletins concentrate on topical and emerging matters, conveying an air of immediacy. In-house media of all types contribute to a sense of unity among personnel.

Comparisons

In deciding on the most appropriate mode of communication, conversation is the least formal and should be considered before the others, but many occasions demand memoranda or letters for defensive reasons. Memoranda vary in length, depending on subject, purpose, and audience; they range from brief notes to dissertations indistinguishable from reports. Since memos are read with great care—with a critical eye, in fact—they deserve meticulous attention to detail in the writing.

Like memos, letters cover a wide range of subjects and purposes. Ordinarily written to outsiders, letters must meet the additional requirements of responsiveness and courtesy. Reports are more or less formal; a later chapter will discuss report formats and the special considerations relating to them. Articles for publication, which may be derived from reports, must make a contribution to their field, and they should be well-written.

Specialized forms of writing have their own purposes, format, style, advantages, and limitations. Minutes of meetings, for example, should convert verbatim transcripts to coherent presentations. Procedure manuals must concentrate on precision at all costs. And despite differences between them, all house organs—magazines, newsletters, and bulletins—are designed basically to pull organizations together.

In a word, when choosing a medium to carry the message, a business writer must be guided by the principle of audience direction and by adherence to a purpose.

3 | *broadened horizons*

Our survey of the field of business writing has so far focused on the kinds of communication that business people engage in routinely. To round out the discussion of media available to business communicators, it remains to explore efforts that reach out beyond the usual audience: writing for publication and speaking before outside groups, the principal methods business writers exploit to advertise themselves and extend their influence. Thus, eager to promote his career, Harry Burns raised his sights beyond the boundaries of his company. Having succeeded in producing effective memos, letters, and reports, he set out to write for a larger readership. Therein lay a test that both challenged Harry and spurred his further development as a business writer.

Credentials and publicity

Why write for trade magazines or professional journals? Answer: To establish *credentials* and to benefit from *public-*

ity. Through his articles, Harry could become recognized as an authority in his field, a spokesman for a group, or a leading advocate of a proposal. He seized the opportunity to gain full credit for his ideas and accomplishments, to become known and respected among colleagues in his industry and his specialty. By making themselves known, good business writers tend to create their own breaks.

Some opportunities would come Harry's way, and others he would generate himself. Once he started to convert portions of reports into articles for submission to magazines—on his own initiative—Harry was asked to contribute articles elsewhere and to speak at meetings. His company wanted him to volunteer for speaking assignments; his name appeared on the speakers' lists of organizations. When he accepted invitations to speak, Harry knew better than to bask comfortably in the limelight; he treated each occasion as a possible fresh impetus to his career. To have acted otherwise would have been a wanton waste of opportunity.

Each of Harry's motives is in accord with the imperative of audience direction. He has promoted himself by satisfying his readers' wants and needs. By orienting his articles to his readers' interests, he has gained an audience. By giving his followers genuine, well-organized material, he has earned a reputation as a thorough analyst. By promoting his talents, he has exploited his potential. In short, there is no conflict between his readers' interests and his own. And as he augments his standing by attracting a select following through his audience-directed approach, he is playing the game according to the rules.

Being published gives Harry visibility. Other persons in business, government, and the professions write articles for the same reason. The question for the ambitious person is not whether to write but what qualities and achievements to put on display. It is not enough merely to publish; everything Harry offers to his readers must redound to his credit. In his efforts to build a suitable image, he can succeed best by striving to perfect certain skills that will speak for his strength of mind and character. Here are a few accomplishments to consider:

◇ *Ability to express oneself well.* At the very least, solecisms must be avoided. Words that don't belong, ungrammatical constructions, and substandard usage can only defeat the purpose of writing. Bombast is always offensive; no one welcomes the misguided attempts of pompous fools to impress people with their exaggerated claims about themselves and their empty rhetoric.

◇ *Knowledge of the subject.* Thoroughly research each subject; carefully select those facts that are relevant, interesting, and unusual; and present the material in ways that indicate depth and breadth of information. By applying a little subtlety, a business writer can convey a lot of knowledge without becoming a bore.

◇ *Logical thinking.* Classify data accurately, so that like things go together and unlike things are kept apart. Be sure the categories are relevant. Each argument must be made to stand on its own as presented, without reliance on relations that have been omitted: readers who are left on their own to bridge the gaps in an argument may fall into the abyss instead.

◇ *Sound judgment.* Everything Harry says or writes provides others with material on which to base their own evaluations of his judgment, and these evaluations rank high among their criteria for making decisions that will affect his career. Hence the importance of reviewing one's own writing critically and correcting even the most trivial slips and transgressions.

Writing and speaking will expose you to critical evaluation, but that should not deter you. Silence may be golden, and reticence may be interpreted by some as an indication of great wisdom, but articulation is the surest route to a position of leadership. Rather than retreat timorously to a hermitage, spend whatever time is needed to acquire the basic skills of business writing so that you will express yourself well on all subsequent occasions. The sooner you acquire these skills, the more time you'll have to cash in on them!

Meeting the standards of general publications brings rewards beyond the credentials and publicity gained thereby in the world outside one's company and circle of acquaintances. Ability to meet the high standards of the better magazines ensures that one's in-house writing will also earn greater recognition for competence. In addition, learning to write well means learning to write easily, and time spent in acquiring good writing habits will be regained many times over.

While learning to write well, one also benefits from the discipline that comes with repeatedly asking such questions as: Why do I believe that? What does it really mean, anyway? Do the facts truly warrant such a conclusion? And the most basic question of all: What is it that I really want to say? Straightening out one's thought processes is what writing disciplined prose has to offer. Few activities can claim to be more intellectually rewarding than that.

Articles and outlets

Many ambitious people recognize the potential of articles as vehicles for gaining reputations and promoting careers for themselves, only to falter at the initial stages of planning. A few suggestions will help those who find themselves in that predicament.

First, draw up a list of possible outlets, including trade magazines and professional journals in your industry and your area of specialization. Don't overlook smaller periodicals put out by local or regional associations; some of these organizations welcome contributions from outsiders. And by all means look into foreign magazines published in English. Excellent publications emanate from Canada, the United Kingdom, Australia, New Zealand, and other countries. You'll be proud to appear in their pages, alongside prominent authors, many of them Americans of stature. Magazines of lesser standing can become stepping stones to your appearance in more notable publications as your own increasing prowess with the pen emboldens your attempts at upgrading the list of media you appear in.

Second, select the most likely magazines for your purposes, after perusal of a few copies of each periodical on your list. Note the coverage, approach, and style preferred by each magazine, and the audience it reaches. Estimate the range of article length, and resolve to help the editors with their problems of space allocation by keeping within that range. In case of doubt about a publication's requirements, ask an editor what he or she looks for. Cooperative editors can be most helpful to authors.

Third, pick a subject you know well from your own experience. Find out what others have written on the subject, and resolve to make a new and individual contribution. Rehashing old stuff won't do much for your standing, even if you find an editor willing to accept such a manuscript. Perhaps no article can be entirely new, but a good article has something to say that goes beyond what has appeared before: additional facts, fresh insights, a challenge to accepted doctrine, an extension of applications, a personal statement. Something to excite the reader's interest.

Fourth, find a device that will appeal to the reader's imagination. Some writers refer to a *peg* or *hook* on which to hang the article, while others speak of an *angle* or a *gimmick*. You can do yourself a favor by thinking instead of a *handle* for readers to grasp as you guide them through the development of your themes, which is what you intend to do in your article.

New writers, eager to publish, are likely to find the search for a suitable handle a difficult and sometimes insurmountable obstacle, and one that is not well understood. However, facing up to a known difficulty will help the aspiring writer to overcome discouragement and despair. Adopt a methodical approach to the task of finding a handle, and you will have taken a crucial further step to your goal.

Some commonly used handles for business articles are based on:

◇ *The how-to approach:* practical articles that tell in detail how to go about doing something.

◇ *The reportorial approach:* factual articles that relate the views of selected interviewees.

◇ *The personalized narrative:* a story told in terms of the experiences of persons with whom readers can identify, and covering situations that readers will recognize in their own activities.

◇ A *sense of urgency:* timely articles that rely on topicality, newsworthiness, and the immediate concerns of readers.

◇ *Logical analysis of research:* theoretical articles that examine data and develop rigorous support for conceptual positions.

◇ A *challenge to myths or fallacies:* polemical articles that attack widely held doctrines.

◇ *The lure of the unusual:* surprise articles exploiting the curiosity value of unexpected results or peculiar happenings.

In considering the possible handles, and in selecting a particular handle for an article, ask what the readers want, what interests them, what will encourage them to continue exploring the subject with you further. Then match your material and the benefits it can offer to your imagined readers—as you imagine they perceive those benefits. Appeals to reader self-interest strengthen a business writer's handle and make it more attractive.

This process of relating the handle to the background and interests of your prospective readers is nothing more than further application of the audience-directed approach, which is central to all writing projects. Once settled on, a proper handle will become an adequate guide in selecting material, constructing an outline, and finding an opener. Moreover, handles that suit both the subject and the wants and needs of the audience are useful not only in all forms of business writing but in business speeches as well.

Fifth, inquire about an editor's interest in the subject and in the handle; and ask for a style sheet, if the magazine encourages you to go forward with your project. Alternatively, you may proceed to gather material, prepare an outline, and write your article. Or you may prefer to try an in-between approach, discussing your project with an editor at one of the intermediate stages, when you are fully conversant with your material or have an outline in hand. Early discussion with an editor can spare you extra work in rewriting later; a competent editor may even be able to offer helpful suggestions for improving your proposed article in the planning stages. Still, the inquiry is optional. You can write "on speculation" and simply submit your completed manuscript to a magazine.

Sixth, follow the customary procedure in preparing a manuscript for submission to a publisher. Double-space on 8½ × 11-inch paper, and allow one-inch margins all around. Retain a copy: the one you submit may not be returned. Send a manuscript to one magazine at a time, to avoid embarrassment. It's even possible that an editor may automatically reject every manuscript bearing your name in the future if he or she has read, evaluated, and accepted one of your pieces only to be told that another editor has acted more quickly.

Early feedback

This method of testing concepts, approaches, and treatments beforehand can be extended profitably. For instance, when Polly Richardson is about to write a memorandum, letter, or report, she saves time and trouble and gathers assurance by trying out her ideas first on the principal reader, a representative reader, or, in a pinch, her boss. The prospective gains are similar to those derivable from consulting with an editor before writing an article for his or her magazine: Polly picks up additional ideas, and avoids having to rewrite later.

Early feedback is best; but whether it comes to her early or late, Polly cannot afford to begin discussing a proposed piece of writing by improvising her thoughts on the spot.

Coming to the conference thoroughly prepared, she offers a proposal that is well thought out; she is ready to defend it even while remaining receptive to suggestions; and she is in a position to discuss the next step, if that should be called for.

Dealing with editors

Unfortunately, not all editors are helpful, imaginative, or even competent. While the business editor who cannot write in standard English is rare, many editors cheerfully admit their inability to write solid pieces for publication outside their own magazines. Worse still are editors who become intoxicated by their sense of power over writers unlucky enough to have ventured into their domain.

When an editor rejects a manuscript, it is unwise either to accept that judgment as the last word or to conclude out of hand that the editor is thoroughly inept. First, submit the rejected manuscript to another magazine. Second, when the manuscript is finally accepted, continue to work with that editor on later manuscripts, and give him or her priority in your plans for further articles. Third, scrutinize whatever comments and suggestions may come from an editor. If they reveal an inferior mentality, or if the stuff accepted by this editor for publication is inadequate, don't waste your time trying to teach this proven incompetent how to do the job right. There are plenty of qualified editors working for business publications, and relatively few incompetents.

It may of course be possible to check out an editor's reputation among other writers. However, a risk is entailed: an author who has been properly rejected may contaminate the thinking of other aspiring writers. Besides, one writer's subject, style, or manner may make him welcome where other capable writers cannot enter. An editor may also be influenced by internal political considerations that few outsiders are aware of. Since there is no need to act on borrowed bad experiences, it is usually desirable to give each editor a chance, and to come to one's own conclusions, based on the treatment one has received.

For their part, editors should act as intermediaries between authors and readers. They represent their readers in their dealings with authors. So long as an editor fulfills that function, there is no cause for writers to complain. It is only when an editor becomes arrogant, pretentious, or petty that writers must defend themselves. The ultimate defense against individually incompetent editors lies in acquiring an ability to write well enough that one's manuscripts will be accepted by other editors. Work at gaining the respect of editors because you have something to say and you know how to say it—that's all you need to get your work published.

One last word on relations with professional editors. Many of them are willing to correct errors, improve style, and even rewrite portions of manuscripts that contain material that is both good and well organized; but few editors will undertake to restructure a poorly organized manuscript, no matter how polished its style may be. The message is clear: *A good outline is the most important single element in getting a manuscript accepted for publication.* Organization of material requires concentrated effort and techniques that will be described in the ensuing chapters.

Speeches and talks

There are many occasions when one must be prepared to speak before a group: in presenting a report orally, in addressing a community organization or a business meeting, in sitting with a panel of experts. Writing skills are indispensable at such times. Although much of what was said previously about written articles and reports will be helpful in preparing a speech, several differences in approach and delivery deserve special consideration.

The basic alternatives for a speaker are writing a complete manuscript to read from, preparing an outline to be used during extemporaneous delivery, and speaking impromptu without aids. In general, free and easy delivery goes over best with modern audiences, whereas reading from a manuscript is least welcome. Such audience preferences create a dilemma for an inexperienced speaker who is timorous about facing a group without a prepared text.

One solution to this problem is to write a speech in advance, taking pains to use less formal language than might be employed in an article, adjusting the phrases to match one's normal conversational style, and then rehearsing the delivery until the words flow naturally. Generally, an article written for publication is not appropriate for reading to an audience. The script must be simplified, and must be dotted with repetition. This revised version should then be read aloud, and the speaker must feel comfortable with it.

After completing his final revisions, Harry Burns marks up the script to indicate inflections, emphasis, short stops, and long pauses (which will give him an opportunity to appraise the audience, his glance moving from face to face). A properly marked script permits concentration on audience behavior during pauses; rehearsal guarantees smoother delivery; and confidence in the compatibility of the material with the interests of the audience helps to capture that audience. The more natural one's delivery—the more nearly it resembles conversational speech—the greater its appeal to a modern audience.

To achieve a truly natural delivery a speaker should learn to speak from an outline instead of a script. As part of his learning process, while endeavoring to acquire total independence from a manuscript, Harry decided to try a half-way approach. He typed the opening statement on a cue card. He also typed the precise wording of essential points and troublesome passages, including transitions. The rest of the material was typed on cue cards in outline format, embellished by key words here and there. On the podium, Harry now found it easier to look out at the audience while speaking—he could pause while referring to his cue cards. Far from being impatient with frequent pauses, audiences prefer them. They contribute significantly to the acceptance of a speaker's style of delivery.

Audience direction is enhanced by attention to messages coming from the audience. Whatever feedback he picks up as he pauses can be used to greatest advantage by the speaker if he remains flexible, and flexibility in adjusting a speech is easier to attain while speaking from cue cards than while reading a complete text. Thus, speaking from cue cards ties in nicely with audience direction.

Harry Burns improves the mileage he derives from his speaking and publishing efforts by recycling his material. When called on to deliver a speech on a topic he is himself permitted to select, he will relate it directly to a field he is familiar with, to work he has been doing, or to a report he has written. With so much material already in his possession, he is spared a great deal of research. Later, after he has given his talk, he incorporates both his original remarks and the question-and-answer material in an article. The task of converting a speech to an article, although its difficulty should not be underestimated, is far less time-consuming than the task of starting on a manuscript from scratch.

Other methods are available for squeezing extra benefits out of material. A talk given to one group may be adapted to other groups merely by changing a few words and allusions to suit the different backgrounds and interests. A full-length article may be divisible into several talks on related subjects, or into brief articles for trade magazines. The audience-directed approach is helpful in converting presentations for use on various occasions and with disparate audiences, thereby stretching the utility of material at hand.

The quest for excellence

The great advantage that writing holds over most other endeavors is visibility of results. Not only does a good manuscript convey a message that the writer has expressed well and thought out clearly, but it also advertises the writer's knowledge and expertise in the fields covered in the manuscript.

However, the extent to which a person realizes the potential of his writing in furthering his career depends largely on the effort that has been devoted to mastering the fundamentals. Business writing has many aspects. Improvement in one aspect may leave a writer struggling with another that is wholly different: knowing how to construct sentences doesn't tell a writer how to develop paragraphs or structure outlines, for instance. So be patient as you concentrate on one phase at a time; the following chapters should be regarded as guides to separate components of business writing, related only insofar as they contribute to the quality of the whole. A great many people are very well able to become good business writers by mastering the parts and then putting them all together.

II | a framework emerges

4 | *collecting input*

The information explosion threatens to overwhelm business writers by surfeiting them with much more material than they can handle. The process of collecting and organizing input is therefore a selective process that requires planning in accordance with certain guidelines that are presented in this chapter.

While still preparing to construct an outline, and before beginning to put words on paper, a business writer must gather information and ideas from her research and experience. Thus the preliminary stages of selecting the type of presentation, identifying the audience, choosing a medium, and finding a handle for the subject are followed immediately by additional planning and preparatory stages in which to collect and organize notes.

Since the purpose of this chapter is to assist business writers in organizing material efficiently, the methods offered will be of greatest help to those who must deal with voluminous notes: in other words, to persons writing reports, articles, speeches, lengthy letters, or complex memoranda. Let it be noted at the outset that procedures must never be allowed to become a straitjacket for the writer; the techniques suggested here should be used primarily as a starting point for adapting those techniques to one's own predilections and circumstances.

It is best to begin with a plan for gathering material. The plan should list sources and set up a crude classification scheme with headings for likely subjects. Creating such a plan involves defining the scope and boundaries of the investigation: the ground to be covered and the methods to be employed.

The breadth of research must of course be sufficient to do justice to the subject. However, there is no point in rehashing material that is already familiar to one's prospective readers. Having made appropriate assumptions concerning the extent of your readers' prior knowledge of the subject, move immediately forward from there. Nor is it practical to explore every ramification of a subject: put a fence around the area to be explored. Also, the maximum length envisaged for a proposed manuscript may become another factor limiting the scope of research. Finally, reporting deadlines may force a time discipline that a business writer ought to apply voluntarily in any case.

Somewhere along the way it will prove useful to bring the subject into focus by selecting a working title for the article. If possible, this working title should reflect subject, handle, purpose, and scope. Since working titles seldom survive editorial preparation of an article for its press run, a writer is free to make these titles as long and as crude as may be convenient. Even cumbersome, dull working titles can do no harm—the outside world will never see them, and they help to hold projects together.

Classification of material

Having settled on the scope of her research, Polly Richardson turns next to methods for classifying material. The key to organizing notes is to select a classification scheme that is suited to the final report or manuscript. Ideally, it would be best to have an outline ready first, so that all notes might be keyed into the headings and subheadings. However, since the final outline is the last thing to prepare before actual writing commences, and the classification process cannot wait for that final outline, Polly proceeds initially by sketching a tentative outline for the sole purpose of hanging a classification code onto it.

It is usually not difficult to come up with a tentative outline at the outset. Anyone who is going to write on a subject must surely be sufficiently familiar with it to conceptualize an approach that will cover most of the bases. Putting the initial concept in outline format helps to structure the thinking and to spotlight gaps. In a pinch, Polly can get herself started by browsing through the literature on a subject or borrowing a table of contents. The tentative outline does not go into detail; there is no need for specific captions; headings and subheadings will serve the purpose well enough. The purpose, of course, is to employ the tentative outline as the basis for a classification scheme.

To illustrate the process of preparing a preliminary outline and classification scheme, take a project that will report the effects of local conditions on the operation of a company's plants around the country. One likely outline might show each location as a heading, with subheadings covering such areas as the labor force, sources of raw materials, transportation, environmental problems, legislation, and taxes.

A classification code that covers both location and topic (heading and subheading, category and subcategory) allows a certain amount of flexibility. Having coded a set of notes LA-RM (for Los Angeles, raw materials), NY-TX (for New York, taxes), SL-EP (for St. Louis, environmental problems), and so on, Polly will be able eventually to sort these notes by location and re-sort them by topic. The re-sorting provides an opportunity to compare structures before settling on the basis for a final outline.

Another way to envision a dual classification scheme is to

run one type of classification across the top of a matrix and the other down the side. In the example above, the headings along the top of the matrix would read *Los Angeles, New York, St. Louis,* . . . , while the captions down the side would read *environment, materials, taxes,* . . . . The dual codes now represent cells within a matrix, and sorting may be by rows or columns.

Re-sorting by alternative classification schemes can be used to spot similarities in the notes and to correlate information in ways that lead to generalization. Just such a process of juxtaposing data and generalizing facts will lead to the discovery of patterns, the development of fresh insights, and the flowering of original concepts. In short, a good classification scheme, with suitable categories for sorting and re-sorting, can be very effective in supporting a creative effort.

Gathering notes

Books and articles should be listed in detail: title, author, book publisher or name of magazine, and date. Polly assigns each source a code letter (A,B,C, and so forth) and writes the appropriate letter on all notes taken from that source. To facilitate sorting and re-sorting, it is advisable to set up a fresh card or page for each note. With access to reproducing equipment, longer quotations may be copied and then pasted on note paper of uniform size and shape for ease in handling.

A writer's own thoughts are always more important in her own project than the ideas of others. As they occur to her, Polly records her thoughts for filing among her notes, setting each idea down, developing it, modifying it, and listing her reservations concerning it. Second thoughts on the same subjects are also important; Polly incorporates these in her notes. The distinctive value of one's writing depends ultimately on one's contribution to extending or illuminating the frontiers of knowledge, providing fresh insights into facts already known, or clarifying difficult concepts for readers. Never lose sight of the need for originality.

Ideas for handles are worth preserving in the form of notes, and also derivative thoughts for constructing transitions from point to point to achieve coherence. Although the earlier discussion of handles was related specifically to articles, any time a handle presents itself as a possibility for arousing interest in a report, memorandum, or any other writing, by all means use it.

To save time later, notes should identify the sources to which quotations will be attributed. Attribution can of course be an honorable gesture acknowledging another's contribution, but on occasion it may be used to avoid responsibility for a questionable statement. *So-and-so said it; I didn't.* At other times, it is simply politic to flatter a source by proffering recognition. It is obviously a hostile act—and will certainly be recognized as such—to quote a passage only to hold the writer up to ridicule. Whatever the motive, permission may be required to reprint a lengthy quotation.

Quotations should always be traced to their origin: it is never a good practice to attribute statements to secondary sources. Sometimes a magazine purports to quote a passage from a book, and then a journal picks up the magazine's version without confirming its authenticity. Attribution to the magazine doesn't relieve the journal of its responsibility if an error should turn up in the quotation, or if the crime of quoting out of context has been committed somewhere else along the line. If a piece is written originally in English, you must go back to the primary source before quoting it in English.

Interviews and surveys

A rewarding method for collecting material is the personal interview. Not only can the guidance and opinions of experts be most helpful to a business writer, but even contrary views can provide a basis for presenting one's own balanced position or for defusing troublesome opposition. Qualified experts in the field can also update a business writer's information and lend currency to her manuscript, especially if these experts can be persuaded to part voluntarily with secrets they have been guarding. At any rate, if a consensus is developing over a controversial topic, it is well to know the facts. And of course the business writer who intends to use a reportorial approach will have to rely on interviews to gather material.

Whenever Polly gathers information by interviewing—and that occurs often—she structures each interview in a way that will ensure that the essential points are covered. The tentative outline and crude classification scheme are useful sources from which to derive the elements of a suitable structure for her interviews. Her planning also permits her the flexibility she needs to follow up new leads, pin down vague comments, demand facts in support of generalities, and trace statements to their sources. To accomplish all these things while retaining the goodwill and cooperation of the persons being interviewed is the essence of the art of interviewing. Anyone who embarks on interviews for the first time will find it prudent to brush up on interviewing techniques beforehand.

A business writer has much to gain and nothing to fear from an interview, for she will ordinarily be talking to a friendly, sympathetic interviewee. Suspicious or uncommunicative persons are known to the rest of the organization; avoiding them and working with helpful persons ordinarily involves no loss of essential material.

Polly calls each interviewee for an appointment ranging from twenty minutes to an hour, and makes it a point to ask for references she can use in preparing for the interview. She is thus provided with material—including definitions and current news—that will equip her to hold her own in the discussion to come. The material may raise questions in Polly's mind or suggest avenues to explore; she brings these to the interview, along with her list of topics to be covered.

During the course of the interview, she explains her mission, telling what kind of material she needs, what purpose she will put it to, in what format her final report or article will appear, and how it will be distributed. She allows her interviewees to wander from the subject; they may thus provide her with new leads or unsuspected viewpoints. She pursues every aspect of a subject that arises, and is especially on the alert for anecdotes that may vivify the end product. In cases of disagreement she assumes she is missing a point somewhere along the way; she follows the interviewee's arguments sympathetically, asking questions designed to clarify rather than contradict the other's opinions. If necessary, she is ready to switch to the role—and attitude—of a reporter trying to get the facts straight for her readers' edification.

When, with Polly's encouragement, the interviewee seems to have talked himself out, two things remain to be done before she closes the interview. First, she goes down her list of topics and verifies that every point has been covered. Second, she asks the interviewee if he has anything more to add; he may want to unveil a whole new facet of the subject. Then, immediately after concluding the interview, she reviews her notes, elaborating where necessary, clarifying obscure points, recalling and adding material that is missing. Only if the set of notes is complete can it be relied on to retain the substance of an interview in its entirety.

In some situations it is necessary to turn for guidance to the statisticians' discipline. To yield valid results a series of interviews or a survey may require selection of a statistically sound sample. The questions used in surveys or interviews should be carefully worded and then tested to eliminate any tendency they may have to influence the respondent toward a desired response or to reflect an unconscious bias of one's own.

In working with questionnaires it is especially important to review every word and be completely satisfied that it carries no unwanted denotations or connotations. No mistakes in sentence structure, grammar, or usage should be allowed to create ambiguity. Simplicity is most important in every question, and the meaning of each answer must be clear.

Selecting material

During the stages of gathering, classifying, and correlating material, a continuous process of evaluation is at work; the business writer is carefully selecting some items, discarding some, and holding others for possible use. In deciding what to include in the finished product, the most obvious criterion is the importance the readers will attach to individual themes. Another fundamental criterion is whether an item is known to the audience. Reciting platitudes is unwise; talking down to a knowledgeable audience will neither ingratiate a business writer nor gain acceptance for what is presented.

On the contrary, the technique of audience direction requires that one estimate the level of knowledge of one's readers, evaluate the understanding they bring to the subject, and predict what facts and opinions they are ready to accept. In short, the business writer cannot avoid making assumptions about her readers, based on the information she has about them. Her safest assumption of course is that they have *not* arrived recently from another planet. Next, she assumes they understand English and have some interest in the subject—otherwise they wouldn't continue reading what she has to say. Now comes the hard question: How much does the audience know? Polly's own assessment of this matter is her only guide. She can hedge a little by establishing a range within which she assumes a large portion of her readers will fall; she may then concentrate on presenting material suitable for readers in that range. Simpler material must be presented with subtlety, so as to inform some readers without patronizing others.

Meanwhile, the selection of material will depend on Polly's evaluation of the audience and its needs. Limits must be set on the amount of detail to be offered and the exceptions to be spelled out. As an illustration, take the familiar rhyme:

Thirty days hath September,
April, June, and November.

All the rest have thirty-one,
Save February, which has twenty-eight alone;
But one year in four
When leap year gives it one day more.

The first two lines are helpful to some people, but hardly anyone would care to hear the remaining superfluous lines. Yet many business reports bore large numbers of readers by indulging in just such foolishness, belaboring what everyone already knows.

In selecting and discarding material, some attention should be paid to two additional considerations. First, since examples and anecdotes are useful in business writing, notes should abound with such material. Second, a surfeit of items may develop in some areas and a relative paucity in others. In the final report, space will have to be allocated to subjects on the basis of relative importance, and never on the basis of availability of material. Thus, in the less important areas, it is wasteful to collect items beyond those that are needed; the search for material should concentrate on the more important areas where items are harder to find.

Digesting the material

Since business readers look disdainfully on mere regurgitation of material predigested by others, the purpose of a business writer's research is not to provide extensive quotations or paraphrases, but rather to provide a starting point from which to synthesize what is known and venture into uncharted regions. The hope is always to discover original concepts.

To this end, Polly examines material gathered from different sources, comparing and contrasting viewpoints, noting areas of agreement and divergence, searching for similarities and contradictions. From this kind of effort she frequently discovers logical patterns that may lead her to unanticipated conclusions. Conceptualizing in new and startling ways is a certain road to gratifying thoughtful readers. Although the reception accorded to such results may be friendly, hostile, or mixed, it can hardly be indifferent.

Sort and re-sort your notes according to several classification schemes and you will find ideas grouping themselves along different lines, bringing to light different sets of relations to explore. The potential gains from this method should not be overlooked. Logic is essentially a matter of classification; logical relations can be expressed in terms of groups that include, exclude, overlap, or are identical with one another; grouping items by essential characteristics is a method for *deductively* acquiring a deeper understanding, and also for *inductively* discovering generalizations. Thus classifying, sorting, and re-sorting material can be relied on as a cogent method for finding logical relations on which to rest a hypothesis or to structure a memorandum or report.

With each sorting of notes, reflect on similarities, differences, analogies, and unusual items that will help you in your search for new meanings. However, two provisos must be observed. First, classification and sorting must rest on genuine attributes, not on superficial, accidental, or trivial properties. Second, a logical hypothesis should be presented only if it describes the known data simply and adequately, for only then will it be acceptable to a discerning audience. Exceptions tend to refute an argument, and a large number of exceptions will destroy a hypothesis altogether.

Organizing the material

Once the facts and ideas have been gathered, classified, sorted, and re-sorted, it is time to select the best approach to a final outline. That approach should relate primarily to the audience. For example, there may be a valid choice for main headings between functional areas and geographical regions. The decision should probably be consistent with lines of command suggested by the company's organization chart. If the action recommended by a memorandum will have to be taken by regional managers, then the outline for the memo should be arranged by region. If functional vice-presidents will make the decisions, then a memo arranged along functional lines is called for. If the presidents of divisions will implement the recommendations, then the outline and structure of the memo should be divisional. Manifestly, in organizing material, the business writer carries audience direction a step forward.

Short memos and letters

Not all writing calls for extensive research or voluminous note taking. Material for shorter memoranda and letters is obviously handled more simply. But it is still advisable to have all the relevant facts at hand and to review them before commencing to write the item. It is also a good idea to group facts and ideas that belong together; this will help keep your reasoning straight and foster discovery of similarities, patterns, and trends.

It is always necessary to establish a logical sequence for presenting ideas. In preparing short pieces, that alone may be all the guidance one needs, and one may be tempted to skip the detailed outlining step; but it is better to resist such temptation. Although short pieces can be written with less attention to the formal methods used for longer pieces, discarding the methodology altogether is unwise, regardless of the length of your writing.

Audience direction in reverse

Political considerations often lead business writers into negative motivations that may pervert the principle of audience direction without destroying it. To put the matter bluntly, a business writer doesn't always want to explain, clarify, or persuade. Sometimes Polly Richardson wants to obfuscate, mislead, or discourage. Her objective may be to withhold information from her audience, rather than to contribute to their store of knowledge.

The writing in these instances is still audience-directed, but the difference in purpose changes the nature of the output. Instead of wanting to do things *for* her readers, Polly now seeks to do things *to* them. Having thus set aside the golden rule, she has freed herself of many obligations and constraints. Paradoxically, the effectiveness of such deception can be further improved by good writing. The process is often denounced because it is often used—and it often works.

Whenever it suits Polly's purposes to obscure issues, she can overwhelm her audience with a flood of trivia, muddy the waters with irrelevancies, and obstruct exploration by piling up the dubious debris of previous ventures. However successful these practices may be in spreading confusion, the basic premise that selection of material must be guided by the business writer's purpose and her evaluation of her audience stands intact. Indeed, expertly conceived tactics only prove the efficacy of audience direction—over and over.

A price must be paid for obfuscation, of course. Careful writing can protect your reputation as a skillful communicator, but faulty logic, poor discernment in separating the wheat from the chaff, or vagueness in presenting your arguments will hurt you among sophisticated audiences. It will become increasingly difficult for you to fool people and also retain their respect. So beware of such cleverness.

5 | *pulling it together*

There is no more effective a time-saver for a business writer than an outline, and no more essential an ingredient of a sound methodology. Serving as a framework on which to hang development and detail, an outline is indeed an indispensable tool for business writers. It ensures that a manuscript will cover every point the writer intends to cover, and that the points will be presented according to a defined pattern. It settles questions of relative position and space allocation, and in addition saves more time than it takes to prepare. Even a casual business writer will find few techniques more useful than the preparation of an outline before proceeding with a report, a letter, a memorandum, or a speech.

Advantages of outlining

Consider the alternatives to outlining: accepting an avoidable risk of losing the audience through a faulty structure they cannot follow, or else restructuring a manuscript after it has been written. Late restructuring, a cut-and-paste job involving previously written paragraphs, is surely more burdensome than shifting captions in an outline before the actual writing commences. Moreover, switches in a completed manuscript involve writing new lead-ins and lead-outs. Rewriting or rearranging a manuscript is an onerous task; it is much easier to settle all structural and logical issues at an earlier stage. An outline is far more amenable to extensive revision than a completed manuscript.

Even a faultless initial structure may subsequently prove to be inferior. Subjects often present alternative possibilities for development, and the first thoughts to occur to a business writer may not prove to be the best methods for developing the subject in the end. Before committing oneself to a particular plan, it is therefore reasonable to take advantage of every available opportunity to explore and experiment with other possibilities; and clearly the most efficient way to conduct these experiments is to construct several outlines for comparison and ultimate selection.

In addition, the act of preparing outlines is in itself a powerful device for self-training, a shortcut to improvement of both written and oral communication. Once Harry Burns learned to think in terms of first introducing a concept and then stating, developing, and restating it before closing his presentation, his effectiveness was greatly enhanced, not only in writing reports or presenting a single thought in a brief memorandum but even when exchanging ideas with others in conversation.

It would be difficult to exaggerate the advantages Harry has gained by subjecting everything he intends to write or say to this discipline of constructing a mental outline in which each remark is prefaced by an introduction. In conversation, that introduction relates to something the previous speaker has said. Picking up from there, Harry makes a statement and follows it up with supporting facts, logical development, illustrations, an explanation, or whatever he has handy. Then he makes a final summation of the theme, and he closes. The more outlining a business writer does, the more quickly the process will become part of his methodology, and the more effectively he will get his message across in all situations.

Before Harry dictates a letter, for instance, he organizes his thoughts in a brief outline. His dictation then proceeds more smoothly than it would have otherwise, with far less backtracking and uncertainty. And when he talks, however briefly, he automatically follows a structured pattern that has become part of his makeup.

For lengthier reports, of course, outlines are indispensable if one is to have any control at all over one's material. And that isn't all: on reaching the point where his ideas are fully ordered in a complete outline and it is time to begin writing, Harry experiences the freedom of being able to develop his thoughts one at a time, without fear of omission or duplication. It is only natural that peripheral thoughts will encroach on the topic at hand, threatening to take Harry off the track in half a dozen different directions, but the existence of an outline keeps him moving in the direction that will best serve his purpose. He can write without being distracted.

Harry may wonder whether readers have been prepared for what they are about to be told. The outline gives the answer: Unquestionably. The plan for the article has seen to that. Now a new idea occurs to Harry and he determines that it ought to be given a place in his report; he forthwith inserts it into the outline at an appropriate point. Eventually it will be given a paragraph of its own.

The question then arises: whether to discuss mathematical modeling at a certain point. Harry again looks to his outline for the answer. If it tells him that this is the time for mathematical modeling, he pursues the subject at once. But if the outline tells him to wait until later, he waits. Having been through the process of thoughtfully constructing an outline and carefully reviewing it, Harry can now reap the benefits of adhering to his previous decisions.

Thus an outline can bestow peace of mind, but only if the business writer learns to rely on it, trusting his own judgment in preparing it. Such self-trust will certainly come if the job of outlining is undertaken seriously, with sufficient time allowed for considering all sorts of alternatives, reworking the outline, and whipping it into a final shape that will deserve the writer's confidence.

An outline can protect a writer from yet another problem that plagues people in business: interruptions. Associates come to Harry with questions that break his train of thought and carry him into wholly different areas for varying lengths of time. Getting back into his writing after each interruption can be exasperating, especially if the associates' calls for help are frequent and the subjects discussed are complex and emotionally or intellectually consuming. An outline can help, provided that it is detailed and reliable. A really good outline permits concentration on one detail at a time, so that, for example, after each interruption, Harry can return to the specific point he had left and can proceed to develop that point almost as though there had been no interruption at all. The greater the burdens a business writer bears, the more important this advantage will be.

Prominent among the benefits derivable from an outline is the freedom it allows to explore each caption with a fresh, uninhibited outlook. Since the relations between a given point and the points that precede and follow it are firmly established by the outline, and since they will not be lost, Harry is free to examine each point in turn as though its existence were independent of the others. Remembering an anecdote that fits, he can use it to lend color to his presentation. Seeing the point in a new light, he may want to digress briefly to make a valid statement that strengthens his report in a special way. Or he can go off on a search for the precise meaning of an idea and for the words that will express it properly. Business writers must expect to be confronted often with ideas that are only half understood, perhaps because business is a pragmatic field virtually unrelated to theoretical disciplines; full comprehension of business phenomena will at times require profound questioning of assumptions. While engaged in such a process, business writers may take comfort in knowing that reentry into more mundane matters—and into the report's basic pattern—will be eased by a carefully constructed outline.

Finally, a detailed outline permits Harry to make an accurate estimate of the length of a speech or article before he writes it. Speakers are often asked to abide by a predetermined time schedule; a simple way to accommodate to this is to time oneself on single points of a detailed outline. An average time per point, divided into the time allotment, will tell the speaker how many captions the *detailed* outline may have.

Similarly, an editor may call for an article of 3,000 words. If experience tells the business writer that his paragraphs average 50 words, then he will need 60 paragraphs; at 75 words to the paragraph, 40 paragraphs will do. In using an outline for these calculations, one need only make it sufficiently detailed that *every caption represents a single paragraph, and every paragraph in the final manuscript is represented by a single caption.*

This useful definition of a detailed outline—one caption equals one paragraph—can be extended so that each heading and subheading stands for a transition paragraph. By employing headings as reminders to insert transition paragraphs, Harry can avoid the appearance of jumping from one point to another. Readers appreciate smooth transitions.

Characteristics of outlines

The preceding remarks on the advantages of outlines have already opened the discussion of their characteristics. The tentative outline described in the preceding chapter is general, comprising only headings and subheadings. By contrast, a detailed outline goes on from there to show individual captions, each of which represents a paragraph of the final manuscript. At this point, other considerations must be explored pertaining to the construction of an outline.

Since nearly every kind of writing contains some instructional content, it is generally useful to pick up the audience at the informational level it has attained and to carry it forward from there, bringing it, in the end, to the point where the business writer wants it to be. The outline should see to it that progress is made from stage to stage on the way. A misinformed audience, however, raises more difficult problems. In handling them, Harry resorts to the same basic strategy, first picking the audience up wherever it is. Without accepting the audience's erroneous beliefs, he can acknowledge them and then immediately proceed to shake and, he hopes, eventually destroy those beliefs that are troublesome.

There is often also a need for persuasive content: a need to sell ideas or conclusions and to prompt people to act on them. A motivational approach—dangling incentives for properly responsive behavior—is favored by marketing people, executives, consultants, and others whose activities center on promoting change by working through others. A motivational outline that should help in meeting this need will be described presently.

Despite these requirements, the essence of all outlines remains: to provide a logical sequence for the arguments presented and the facts that support them. Although persuasion is frequently loaded with emotional content, persuasion and logic need not conflict with each other. People are both rational and emotional, and it is possible to appeal to both aspects of human nature in the same report. In any case, the outline must be predominantly logical.

Outlines are well suited to serve another function: assigning positions and allocating space to topics. Readers are entitled to infer that the first point in the outline is the most important, and that points decline in importance from there on. They are also entitled to infer that a point discussed in five paragraphs is more important than a point covered in three. Thus, within a segment of a report, and in other communications as well, points should generally be made in the order of their importance. Also, space should be allocated to points according to their relative importance. It is much easier to settle these matters before actual writing commences. In other words, these issues of position and space allocation should be put to rest while the outline is being prepared by the business writer.

The notes at last having been sorted and re-sorted; and trial outlines having been constructed to reflect the various approaches; and one outline having been selected, revised, modified, and reviewed; and a single structure having been settled on—it must be expected that the initial scheme for classifying notes no longer resembles the final, detailed outline. Rather than recode all the notes, it is simpler at this point to locate the code designations originally assigned to the material and record them alongside each new heading and subheading. This type of cross-indexing leads Harry Burns straight to the appropriate material as his writing proceeds from topic to topic.

Structure of reports

In a general way, business reports follow one of two basic formats, depending on the nature and purpose of the report and the inclinations of the author. Both formats order facts and arguments logically. The difference lies in the writer's view of his readers' needs and his sense of his own purposes.

The first, expository format combines logical and historical approaches, beginning with the authorization for the study and the reasons for undertaking it—those reasons perhaps including a description of symptomatic conditions. That is followed by an explanation of the methodology the writer has employed to establish the authenticity of facts and findings and to gain credibility for the conclusions reached. The facts and findings are then enumerated before the discussion turns to analysis and definition of problems or issues. Next, possible solutions are considered and are either accepted or rejected. Finally, the report announces recommendations that arise out of the study along with benefits that may be gained by following the recommendations. The status of the subject may be discussed in its historical perspective, along with a prospectus of work that remains to be done.

Variations on this expository pattern are frequently used by internal committees or study groups and by scientific, engineering, and development personnel. Outside consultants also use it, but many, perhaps most, management consultants prefer a motivational pattern.

This second, motivational format follows the opening with a summary of recommendations and benefits—the things most likely to interest the busy reader. It then proceeds to the rationale for accepting one set of solutions while rejecting others. It continues by supporting its analysis with facts and findings. Methodology may be described next or may be covered in an appendix—an appropriate place for a description that is technical, involved, or lengthy. The report concludes with a restatement of recommendations and immediate steps to be taken. Historical perspectives are consigned to an appendix.

The logic of the motivational format proceeds pretty much in reverse order to the logic of the direct format, as it attempts first to establish reader interest and then to maintain it. As an added benefit, the motivational format permits busy readers to drop off at a number of points, depending on the depth of their interest. Action-oriented executives may be pleased to find that recommendations and benefits come early in the report. Those who want to know why a particular recommendation has been made can find answers in later pages, while less inquisitive minds can stop without missing the essential results of the study. Those who demand supporting evidence for an argument can read on, while those who lack such an interest have at least read the argument the report develops. Finally, the technically oriented or highly critical reader can find details of the methods employed in the study. Since few readers are genuinely interested in these details, they are consigned to a less conspicuous position. Thus the motivational format avoids the risk of losing busy readers before they ever get to the parts they would be interested in.

The principles behind the two basic formats—expository and motivational—are applicable to all reports. These approaches to outlining must be borne in mind whenever a business writer arrives at the point of building a structure for a report of any kind.

Article formats

Reports of studies are often easily converted to manuscripts of the *how-to* or the *what-to-do-about-it* varieties. Here is a sample rough outline for a how-to article:

◇ An introduction that describes symptomatic conditions that led to the call for a study.
◇ Analysis of underlying causes and real problems, limiting the exposition of details in order to hold the interest of a wide audience.
◇ Discussion of possible solutions, emphasizing the rationale behind the acceptance or rejection of each.
◇ Implementation problems, frankly disclosed, along with a description of efforts to overcome them.
◇ Outcome, including benefits and disappointments.

The what-to-do-about-it format is more readily adaptable to the presentation of a composite case study, with some resemblance to a style of reporting that weaves a story around factual material:

◇ An introduction that presents either a problem or the symptoms of one.
◇ Description of remedies proposed and solutions attempted unsuccessfully, with details of experiences and analysis of the reasons for failure.
◇ The successful approach in theory and practice: the solution that works.

Outlining techniques

It would be wasteful to concern oneself with the appearance of an outline. Since no one but the business writer himself is ever going to see it, any effort expended on esthetics is lost.

Nor is there any need for consistency or parallelism in the way captions are written. If a single word will suffice to recall a point later, whereas a longer phrase is needed for another point, then use whatever will serve your purpose best. More important, if a full sentence occasionally occurs to Harry, exactly as he wants it to appear in the finished product, he finds it easier to write it out immediately than to condense it first and reconstruct it later. If his outlines come up as a jumble of words, phrases, and sentences, no one but Harry will ever know, and he suffers no harm—provided of course that the meanings are clear, and every entry is in its proper place.

Sometimes, however, Harry finds himself preparing an outline for submission to a group he is working with or to his boss. If cryptic notations will mystify these people, then he must provide captions that are understandable. In such cases, a most useful outline comprises full topic sentences, each to be developed into a paragraph. Such an outline permits co-workers to read what is written with comprehension and to comment intelligently; it avoids misunderstandings concerning the intended text; and it carries forward the job of writing, while facilitating the later stages.

Reviewing an outline

Having completed his outline, Harry reviews it with regard to all the matters discussed above, raising such questions as these:

⋄ Is the outline consistent in following either an expository or a motivational approach? Is the overall pattern reasonable?

⋄ Do the major points follow a logical sequence, or do they skip around? Is any major point out of place? Are the most important points made early?

⋄ Does the reasoning proceed smoothly from point to point, or do gaps in the argument remain to be filled in?

◇ Within each section, does the strongest, most important point come first, followed by the second strongest? Or is rearrangement within sections called for?

◇ Does any section need to be strengthened by an infusion of material or a tightening of the logic?

◇ Are all essential points covered? Have the purposes been accomplished?

◇ Is the allocation of space proper, or should adjustments be made by adding captions under important headings or deleting captions from less important headings that threaten to run too long? Similarly, does the overall length meet existing constraints?

III | writing methods

6 | *gates and bridges*

Having put together a detailed outline, Harry Burns is ready to begin writing. As we've defined it, a detailed outline is a logical sequence of headings, subheadings, and captions, each calling for development into a paragraph. In particular, the introductory heading asks for an opening paragraph, and the other headings and subheadings require transitions. This chapter looks closely at openings and transitions, the gates and bridges of a writer's journey.

Openings for business writers

Too many people sit down with every intention of writing, only to find themselves staring endlessly at a blank page. To aggravate a bad situation, too much attention is paid to the symptom while the cause is neglected. The blank page is not the enemy; the problem lies in having come to the job unprepared. Yet there are people who curse the blank page with the zeal of a demon frustrated in his campaign to sully virginal purity.

Out of this phobia a trick method for getting started has evolved. To replace staring, this method would have a business writer set pen down on paper and scribble whatever irrelevant thought comes to mind, like this: *Seated at my desk and looking out the window, I can see. . . .* Some followers of the method find that they're ready to write seriously after a brief warm-up. Let's not argue with their success.

Nevertheless, it's reasonable to venture an assault on the roots of the problem. Stated bluntly, if a business writer finds himself unable to begin writing, then he hasn't completed his preparation. Here's why: All he needs to provide himself with an opener is a view of the audience (which he should have adopted when he contemplated doing his report, letter, or memorandum) or a handle (which he should have found initially, when he framed his concept in terms that could appeal to the audience). Harry Burns's opening statement reaches out to the people he intends to capture, if not captivate; hence the proper bait for him to hold out is a forthright announcement of what the reader can expect to find in the piece. For example, if Harry is going to explain how to speed up collections of receivables, he can open with a statement of the principal benefit: *Reducing your investment in receivables can save your company money.* Or, *One company saved $50,000 in interest costs by improving its collections from customers.* Or a keep-up-with-the-Joneses appeal, *Leading companies rely on sophisticated techniques for managing their collections.*

These openers enable a reader to answer the question, "Should I read on?" The rest of the opening paragraph will tell the reader more about the subject. By the end of that first paragraph, readers will know that the manuscript is going to describe methods for approving credit, monitoring receivables, and collecting open accounts. Thus, readers have been told what Harry is writing about (the subject) and why they might be interested (the benefits). Harry could also stretch the point by indicating who will use his methods and where (credit and collection personnel in their department), but why bother with such superfluities merely to conform to a neat pattern of who, what, where, when, why, how? For Harry's manuscript, as for a great many others in business, it is sufficient to open with the what and the why. Although the six journalistic questions—who, what, where, . . . —provide a useful checklist, they do not constitute a formula for all openers.

Actually, an opener can be a simple statement: *This is a report on pension plans and deferred profit sharing among companies in our industry.* Such an opener may lack punch, but it does the job. Alternatively, a newsy approach may be injected: *Companies in our industry have modified their pension and profit-sharing plans significantly in recent years.* A reference to causal factors can be more forceful: *Legislation in recent years has had a marked effect on pension plans in our industry.*

Personalized openers are often preferred. For instance, a summary of the literature on absenteeism might open thus: *If you are plagued by absenteeism, recent studies may shed light on your problem.* An action-oriented approach might read, *You can do something about absentees in your department.* The subject can be raised as a question or a series of questions: *Does absenteeism plague you? Can you do something about it?* Opening questions rely on shock effect to some extent and are easily overdone; perhaps one question is enough: *Does absenteeism plague you? Well, now you can do something about it.*

Suppose a report or article advocates flexitime, and absenteeism is only a secondary issue. The writer may be tempted to lure readers on the pretext that the subject is absenteeism, but the ruse won't work. A better opener would be, *Flexitime may be the answer to some of your problems*—for example, absenteeism. It's all right to throw out an aspect of the subject with strong audience appeal, but it's still necessary to stay with the proper subject.

A good opener reaches out to those particular business readers who will gain something from the manuscript by offering them a harbinger of what they may expect. That harbinger must above all be genuine. It must not offer more than will be delivered, or offer something the manuscript doesn't cover. In a word, *the opening must never cheat the reader*. A deceptive opener can have only disastrous consequences: it drives away the natural audience while enticing the wrong readers. Since the deceived ones will desert rather quickly, and those who were lost initially will not return, such openers lose both groups.

The best openers contain an unspoken invitation to read on. To attract and hold initial interest, they are delivered with some punch and are not permitted to run too long. The first draft of an opener says what has to be said in a sentence of moderate length. When the entire piece is finished and revision begins, the opener is rewritten until it is crisp, light, and lively. Later chapters in this book tell how that's done.

The opening paragraph should be shorter than your own average paragraph. When an opening paragraph runs too long, break it up—artificially, if that's the only way (something you wouldn't do elsewhere). The second paragraph should also be short. Hang on to the allure of the opening by building up to longer paragraphs slowly.

To summarize, an opener announces the subject and indicates the approach to it. If that approach is directed toward the proper audience, then the opener will appeal to the right readers naturally. A wide variety of statements and questions may be devised to carry the opening message. Whichever type of opener is selected, it cannot go wrong if it presents each reader with enough material to answer the question, "Should I go on reading?"

Openings for business speakers

A listening audience differs from a reading audience in that listeners make their choice—to attend or not—beforehand. To a great extent, listeners are captives who—perhaps out of ordinary courtesy—will not walk out if the opener fails to grab them, or the rest of the talk falls short of inspiring or inflaming them as they would have wished. They are more likely to stay in their seats and resent the speaker. They will doubtless also absent themselves in large numbers the next time that speaker is scheduled to appear.

Since listeners don't walk away at the end of the first sentence—in contrast to readers, who often do move on to other things if the opening sentence turns them off—Polly Richardson feels a greater freedom in selecting her opening remarks for a speaking engagement. She can spend some time at the outset building up her audience's interest, ingratiating herself, making people want to listen to her. She can concentrate on promoting her acceptability, on raising the audience's expectations of an entertaining talk, or on promising to deliver an informative speech, one worth listening to. In other words, she may use her opening remarks to charm the audience with her personality, delight them with her wit, or whet their appetite by describing what is to come.

Polly finds that her personality comes through best when she behaves naturally on the speaker's platform. Because so many speakers are stiff, formal, and dull, it is always refreshing to an audience to observe one who is not afraid to present herself as she is. Light humor, a few witty remarks, or a relevant story can win over an audience, but sophisticated listeners seem to become impatient with jokes unrelated to the topic. The obligatory amusing story of years past may still be used to warm up an audience, or to make it forget the previous speaker and his orientation, but a speaker should feel perfectly free to forgo the opening joke if it seems advisable to do so.

Although Harry Burns likes to plunge right into his subject, he finds it advantageous to begin slowly, allowing his audience time to adjust to him. He repeats important phrases and whole sentences, to make sure they sink in. To keep his audience on the right track before he picks up momentum, he avoids rapid talk at the early stages. Rather than jolt his listeners, he allows them to get their bearings while at the same time receiving a large portion of his message.

Whichever style of opening a speaker adopts, it is always a good idea to project a friendly tone, a light touch, a firsthand knowledge of the subject, and an eagerness to share the store of valuable information with others. The opening creates the initial impression and sets the mood; it should therefore be in keeping with the rest of the talk and not a thing apart.

Transitions

Transitions between major segments of a manuscript have something in common with openers, in that they prepare the reader for what is to follow and are designed to hold the reader's interest at the same time. If an opening in a manuscript is analogous to an initial approach to a person in ordinary business dealings, then transitions touch base regularly afterward, relating each segment to the central theme and bringing coherence to the whole. It is also appropriate to view both openers and transitions in terms of handles. The opener rests on the primary handle for the manuscript, and transitions can rely on auxiliary handles related to the main handle, but adapted more specifically to their respective sections. This view perceives a transition as telling the reader why he should want to read on.

Yet a transition does more than merely introduce a section of a report: it bridges the gap between sections, relating the next section to what went before. Because an outline presents subjects in a logical order, a business writer ought not to suffer any pain in devising such bridges. Just don't overlook the need for them; they serve an important purpose.

A speaker can always use the device of recapitulating where he has just been and where he is now, and combine this with a projection of where he is headed next. Such transitions tend to be long, which limits their usefulness in written reports and articles; but they accomplish something worthwhile for speakers.

Another technique is to split the transition into a lead-out planted in the closing paragraph of one section and a lead-in picking up at the beginning of the next section. The lead-out and lead-in may be easily tied together in one of several ways, the simplest being restatement of an idea. The lead-out closes one section with a summary of its contents and suggests its connection with the next section; the lead-in then follows up with a statement introducing the next section and suggesting its connection with the one just concluded. Except for a shift in emphasis, the lead-out and lead-in are stating twice what is essentially the same thought.

To illustrate, the final sentence of a section on budget construction might read: *When volume forecasts have been completed and costs have been estimated, the budget becomes a tool for controlling operations.* The next section then opens this way: *Operations are controlled by comparing actual volumes and costs with previously budgeted figures.* The carry-over from lead-out to lead-in need not always be as elaborate as a restatement of an entire thought; it often suffices to throw out a phrase and then pick it up, or simply to echo a significant word, as was done in the illustration above.

We've been discussing transitions between sections, where it's important to hang on to one's readers while passing through a bend in the road, where centrifugal tendencies may pull people away tangentially. Such transitions generally require full paragraphs for development. Within a section, however, the centrifugal pull is weaker; transitions from one subsection to another are therefore customarily less elaborate. It is still a good idea to use a full transition paragraph for most subsections, but occasionally a sentence or two will do the job well enough. Similarly, in moving from one paragraph to another within a subsection, a single sentence should suffice to make the transition smooth.

These transitional sentences will follow the methods spelled out above for lengthier transitions.

Connectives

There is a need also to tie sentences together within paragraphs, and this need is fulfilled in two ways. The topic sentence provides a unifying theme, and transition words signal the direction to follow. It is most helpful to a reader to be forewarned at the beginning of a sentence whenever the business writer intends to make a U-turn. Thus Polly starts such a sentence with *however, but, by contrast, contrariwise, nevertheless, yet, on the other hand, still, despite, notwithstanding.* A curve in the road should be signaled by a connective word less contradictory; for example, *actually, realistically, at the same time, interestingly, unexpectedly, unaccountably, perhaps, or.* Concessions and limitations may be noted by *sometimes, to be sure, possibly, to some extent, conceivably.* An aside should be introduced by *incidentally, digressing, analogously.*

Even when you intend to stay on course, you can help your readers by notifying them that you are moving ahead in the same direction. Signal your intention with a word like *additionally, and, also, besides, moreover, furthermore.* Comparisons are announced with *similarly, likewise, in the same way.* If you want to lend the appearance of strength to an assertion, *indeed, in fact, certainly* may help. Words like *undoubtedly, surely, seemingly* are sometimes used to raise doubts instead of setting them to rest. Importance can be signaled by *significantly, notably, remarkably;* and primacy by *chiefly, mainly, principally.* Illustrative cases are introduced by phrases like *for example, for instance, to illustrate.* In presenting a logical argument, words like *whereas, granted, since, thus, hence, therefore, consequently, necessarily* come to mind. *Accordingly, implicitly, by inference, this suggests* are less rigorous.

Some connectives indicate temporal relations: *then, next, later, afterward, before, earlier, previously, sooner.*

Words like *obviously, patently, manifestly, clearly* are frowned on by some editors on the quibbling grounds that anything obvious should not be stated; actually, we must often say the obvious, either to carry along the less informed readers, to make certain that all readers are thinking along the right lines, or to lead up to a more difficult concept. Then there are phrases like *from another standpoint, more simply, in the view of certain experts*—these convey their own message. Numbering statements *one, two, three* or *first, second, third*—and there should be consistency in the use of one series or the other—lends cohesiveness to a piece of writing. Such words as *finally, lastly, in conclusion* help to emphasize the last point in a series; while *to summarize, in short, summing up* introduce a restatement of points covered previously.

In sum, a courtesy that readers find most beneficial is a word or phrase inserted at the beginning of a sentence to indicate the direction about to be taken. Such a connective helps to guide readers in their thinking and keeps them where the business writer wants them to be. A large store of connectives will serve well. Start with the illustrative words and phrases enumerated above, consciously employing them so often that their use becomes habitual.

The only danger in the free use of connectives and transitions lies in a breach of promise. Once having indicated his intentions, the only honorable course of action for a business writer is to carry through. The carelessness that allows a person to write *however,* followed by a restatement of his thought, destroys the usefulness of the connective. Similarly, an apparent lead-out that is not picked up in the following section can lead only to bewilderment. It may seem like a great idea to close a section with, *Hardships will be encountered along this route; there will be obstacles to overcome;* but the next section had better describe some of those hardships and obstacles or readers will be entitled to feel they've been misled. Never say, *The matter doesn't end here* if in fact it does; readers, because they can't talk back, become frustrated by such contradictions.

Closings

Just as an opening is a form of transition—from whatever occupied the reader before he took up the manuscript—a closing may be likened to another transition. The closing will at least be read in virtual contiguity with a transitional act on the part of the reader as he sets the report or article down, so it is not unreasonable to include a discussion of closings in a chapter that covers openings and transitions.

The best closings wrap up themes covered previously. In composing a close, remember that readers perk up when the end is near, and busy readers in particular often turn directly from the beginning to the end of an article or report, either skimming or skipping all that lies between.

The close offers the last chance to get your message across. The parting shot will be remembered more vividly than the rest of the piece. Accordingly, it behooves the business writer to formulate the main argument strongly and succinctly in the final pitch. Summarize what has been said; reiterate the conclusions previously demonstrated. Call the closing a summary, if that's what it is; a conclusion, if that designation is appropriate; a summary and conclusion only if both terms are applicable. Never present new material or raise new issues in closing; nor is it permissible to toss in a gratuitous remark unrelated to what preceded it. An exit is no time to hint about subjects not previously discussed; that practice can only bewilder and frustrate your readers. Rather, use the closing to reinforce what has already been said. And especially in letters and memoranda, the closing is the place to make sure the audience is plainly told what you want it to do, if action is to be taken.

The central theme that runs through a discussion of openings, transitions, connectives, and closings is concern for the reader. This concern is well summarized in the recurrent phrase *audience direction*. In the end, the gates and bridges are for the use of the readers; the journey is theirs as much as the author's.

7 | *developing an idea*

Every idea has to be sold to the audience. That is basically why each caption in the detailed outline must be developed into a full paragraph of its own. A detailed outline thus becomes in effect a list of ideas to be unfolded in a prescribed sequence.

The function of a paragraph

The "one caption, one paragraph" rationale depends on the primary function of a paragraph as the vehicle for developing an idea. As everyone has been taught since childhood, a sentence is the *expression* of a thought. The *development* of a single idea from a caption will require several additional thoughts—additional sentences—in a paragraph. In other words, the bare expression of a thought is the function of a sentence; in a paragraph, the topic sentence carries the central thought, and development of that thought is the function of the rest of the paragraph.

Polly Richardson never allows herself to forget that it's

the duty of a business writer to unfold her ideas properly, so that an intelligent and reasonably diligent reader can follow her thinking. Any time a business writer throws out an idea and fails to develop it, she imposes a burden on her readers, requiring them to supply what she has neglected to give them. This transfer of responsibility runs the heavy risk of misdirecting readers and even losing them altogether. In addition, given the climate of intense politicking that characterizes organizations of all sorts, certain unscrupulous interpreters of terse and cryptic remarks won't shrink from claiming a share of the credit—and very likely the lion's share—for having discovered hidden applications the writer was either not aware of or not clear about and that other readers completely missed. Hence, business writers with something to say owe it not only to their readers but to themselves to develop every idea unequivocally.

Readability

It requires conscious effort to unfold ideas properly, and a methodology for developing paragraphs is presented later in this chapter. But Polly has a more urgent reason for contriving ways to develop each idea in turn rather than skip too soon to the next idea. This second reason is linked to readability.

Polly's readers will find it difficult to stay with her report unless they are given time to digest each idea as it is served up to them. How can they be given the required time? Inserting blank spaces won't do it. Readers need additional words; these can be supplied by repetition, development, or pleasantries.

Another reason for adding words is to improve the rhythm, which is an important factor in readability. "Unnecessary" words—expletives such as *there are*—can be useful as devices for improving the rhythm without damaging the leanness of style that is essential in business writing.

Friendliness and courtesy are always valued highly by readers. A few polite words can serve to relieve the starkness of overly terse writing. There may even be a place for bland phrases on occasion, although these can accomplish only a minor purpose and virtually subvert the main goal of serious writing. In order to make the added words count for something, it is better to offer readers solid substance than to woo them with sweet little nothings. But that solid substance must of course enhance readability—otherwise it is better left out.

Be especially wary of weighing the manuscript down with ambiguous verbiage. Added words sometimes have a way of intruding extraneous thoughts that are capable of leading an audience astray. When that happens, the effectiveness of a paragraph can be destroyed. Consider this quotation: *Certified public accountants must retain their independence. When a CPA firm undertakes to provide management advisory services, the firm's specialists are assigned to help their client's management. Clearly, these same specialists could not perform an audit of management at the same time.*

The phrase *at the same time,* tacked on gratuitously, raises a spurious issue. The proper issue is preservation of independence, and not physical limitations that prevent the simultaneous performance of two separate tasks.

Terseness, then, can be overdone; and a few words inserted here and there can improve readability. But as far as possible, words should be made to count for something. Above all, added words must not distract an audience from the main argument.

Repetition and restatement

Repetition and restatement can help to carry an audience along. Whenever an unfamiliar but useful bit of terminology comes up, repetition helps readers become accustomed to the strange words. After introducing a novel thought, Polly restates it—several times, if necessary—and she may even present the new concept from different viewpoints. Repetition is a recognized teaching technique, a highly effective method for putting a new idea across. Repeat a thought as often as necessary, without fear and without qualms.

An audience of listeners is even more dependent on repetition than readers are. In speaking, Harry Burns doesn't hesitate to repeat a sentence or a phrase verbatim. When he has said something that is unfamiliar to the audience and it responds with blank, uncomprehending stares, he stops and repeats what he has said, pausing as necessary to let the thought sink in. He slows down his delivery to give his audience time and to alleviate the strain of having to remain continuously attentive. There is no way that a listener can avoid wandering occasionally, and those who have had no previous exposure to a subject may have difficulty finding their way back. Repetition can help a speaker to round up these strays.

Although repetition and restatement certainly have their place, they must not be abused. Be sure the problem is reader unfamiliarity with the subject, and not your own failure to express your meaning properly. Too often a writer makes several attempts to clarify a statement simply because her first try was poorly done. The result is more likely to irritate and confuse readers than straighten things out for them. When a business writer finds herself restating a thought because she is dissatisfied with the way it reads, then it is time for her to scratch out what she has written and make a fresh start. The primary requirement is to work over the faulty statement until it says what the writer intends. Only then can a proper decision be made as to whether restatement is necessary.

How much restatement should a business writer employ? An audience obviously needs less time to absorb familiar material than a strange subject or novel treatment, but the need never vanishes entirely. Perhaps the message itself is not really new, but it is presented differently: some reiteration is useful to hold the audience's attention against all distractions. A considerate business writer recognizes her audience's need for time to digest each thought. The most satisfactory way to provide an opportunity for improved comprehension is to develop every thought into a proper paragraph. Thus it is essential to have a variety of methods available for developing these paragraphs.

Development methods

It should be obvious by now that writing is not a single subject but a whole collection of subjects of varying degrees of importance. Among the elements that rank at the top—the critical elements—is paragraph development. Fortunately, many development methods are available. The following catalog of frequently used methods will permit business writers to systematically approach the job of selecting a particular method for each paragraph, based on such considerations as the kind of topic it deals with, the nature of the material at hand, the requirements imposed by logical development of a theme, and, most important of all, the needs of the audience.

The methods of restatement and repetition have already been discussed. Close relatives are the methods of definition, explication, and illustration. In turn, these methods frequently entail descriptions of limits, exclusions, modifications, or prerequisites. Sometimes comparisons or contrasts flow naturally. The purposes of all these related methods may be to elucidate a point, to refine a statement, to translate technical jargon, to remove apparent inconsistencies or anomalies, to provide perspective, to vivify or corroborate readers' experience by the use of examples, or to enrich the presentation with background or illustrative material drawn from the field of inquiry. A few examples will suffice to indicate how these methods can be used to develop paragraphs designed to win the confidence of an audience.

⋄ *A computer can "learn" by noting relations and accumulating experience. Recognition of patterns can lead the computer to expect certain results. For example, with adequate data and programming, a computer could* "*learn*" *that a given company makes no sales on Sunday. Furthermore, if the company subsequently changes its policies, the computer could report Sunday sales as an exception to what it had expected.*

◇ *The complexity of modern organizations demands planning and coordination of activities. It would not do to spend fortunes promoting a product, only to find that the company's plants are not equal to the task of meeting the demand that is generated. It would not do to schedule equipment to produce parts, only to find that there are not enough assembly lines to put the parts together. It would not do to hire and train production workers, only to find that shortages of materials leave them with nothing to work on. The need for coordination exists between departments and within departments at all levels. Coordination and planning.*

◇ *Many auxiliary functions will reflect in more or less subtle ways the implications of organization structure. A credit department operating under marketing auspices will have a different frame of reference from one operating under the chief financial officer. A personnel department with its own vice-president will look at many issues differently from one that reports to the treasurer or general manager.*

◇ *The systems department, as a staff activity, services the line operations. When a production supervisor needs help in eliminating bottlenecks, or customer complaints indicate problems in scheduling, a systems analyst may be assigned to study the situation and report his conclusions. However, systems personnel never attempt to implement solutions themselves, nor do they usurp the authority of line managers. In assisting line personnel, the systems department may proffer advice, but it cannot issue orders or instructions on its own. Only line managers can do that.*

◇ *Criteria for satisfactory return on investment may vary markedly between individuals in the management ranks of a company. To put it in the simplest terms, one executive may be willing to take great risks in the hope of earning large profits; another sees the company's best hope in taking the course that involves the least risk while offering prospects of a satisfactory return; and a third would multiply the expected return by the probability of realizing it for each alternative investment, in order to select the proposal that offers the highest probable value per dollar invested. In planning and decision making, maximizing profits may mean different things to different people.*

Another group of development methods seeks to expound or support the logic of the topic sentence by marshaling evidence, enumerating actual or possible causes or effects, exploring the significance of items or relations between items through analogies, persuading by reinforcement of claims, exhorting by stress on urgency or cogency, or convincing by recourse to authority. A few illustrations of these methods will suffice.

◇ *There are many reasons why collections lagged during the period. Lowered standards for granting credit probably increased the number of slow-paying customers. Delays in processing invoices and statements caused customers to pay later than usual. High interest rates influenced prompt-paying customers to withhold remittances until they came due. And a business slump affected other customers adversely.*

◇ *Faulty receiving procedures can be costly. They may result in paying for goods never received or received in poor condition, accepting inferior substitutes, and continuing to deal with unreliable suppliers. Additionally, defective material may come to light during late stages of processing, resulting in rejection, rework, or scrap. And if defects are not caught in the finished product, customer returns and loss of goodwill must be expected.*

◇ *A profit plan must stand on a clearly defined statement of purpose. Before you can map out a trip, or even a seg-*

ment of a journey, you must choose your destination. Only then can you proceed to select a route. Similarly, when a company undertakes to chart its future course, it must first establish its objectives. It must know where it wants to go.

In business writing, paragraph development may follow a pattern that is temporal, geographic, or organizational. Thus a history of events is often useful to demonstrate an evolutionary pattern or to augment understanding of a current situation; or a timetable for contemplated actions is just what the occasion calls for. At other times, descriptions of diverse local characteristics, market segments, or kinds of activity are most appropriate; or departmental attributes within a company may provide precisely the kind of development best designed to carry readers along the road selected for them. Again, a few illustrations will suffice.

◊ Our line of disposable products has suffered declining sales and profits for several years. After an initial wave of interest, consumers began to find fault with the products. Then old-line competing items were improved in ways that tended to offset the advantages previously enjoyed by disposables. Growing ecological concern further hampered the disposable line. More recently, price increases on raw materials have accentuated a profit squeeze.

◊ We continue to make substantial progress in our efforts to reduce air pollution. Scrubbers installed in the Northeast region are now operating. Our recently constructed plant in the Midwest pretreats fuel. An experimental process has successfully completed its tests in the Southern region, while encouraging results in the Far West have led us to plan additional installations there.

◊ A series of seminars will bring the new concepts to people in all parts of the country. Beginning in Los Angeles in January, a team of discussion leaders will go to Dallas in February and Atlanta in March. After a respite for revising and updating, the group will then go on to Baltimore, New

York, and Boston in the spring. Finally, meetings in Detroit and Chicago will be scheduled for next summer.

Choosing a method

With all these methods to choose from, the process of developing a paragraph to suit the topic sentence should not be overly difficult. The choice of a particular method is sometimes dictated by the material at hand: data from plant locations or a historical record suggest geographic or temporal development. Sometimes the overall method for developing a theme calls for a statement of causes at specific points; or consistency with the rest of an exposition may require a departmental pattern, even if additional data must be gathered for the purpose.

At all times, however, the needs of the readers should remain the primary consideration. Polly Richardson selects a departmental pattern only when her readers are characterized by departmental concerns. She accumulates data by geographical location when preparing to write for readers who will welcome a geographical pattern of presentation. With adequate planning, chance factors are minimized—and the reader always comes first.

In some of the illustrations above, different development methods were combined in a single paragraph. Is it advisable to mix methods that way? Yes. Ordinarily, it is feasible to combine two or three related methods of development. Definitions, illustrations, and limits go well together. Results, causal factors, or predictions frequently fit into a chronological pattern. Logic and persuasion are linked by common bonds. But a paragraph begins to confuse the reader when it goes off in too many directions at once. When Polly has defined and illustrated a topic in one paragraph, she prefers to go to a new paragraph to make her analogies and comparisons.

There are times when a presentation can be improved by adding material to it. First, when more space is allocated to a topic than the accumulated material can support, Polly tries to develop an additional paragraph along different lines, digging out new material to meet specific needs. She may have offered an illustration and an exception; with more illustrations and more exceptions, she can split the exceptions off into another paragraph. Second, an occasional topic sentence may deal with a weak subject, little more than a truism. A bald statement and restatement can hardly be expected to excite enthusiasm among readers. Perhaps nothing else will either, but a business writer can try to hold the interest of her readers with an anecdote, an unusual application or limitation, a novel extension—something different, something intriguing.

8 | *blending and unfolding*

A paragraph is a collection of sentences unfolding a single idea. The preceding chapter enumerated methods for developing an idea. Next, the structure of paragraphs must be understood—for the parts of a paragraph are blended into a unified entity whose purpose is to hold interest, make a point, and carry the audience along.

The central idea and the topic sentence

No principle is more important in constructing a paragraph than the unfolding of a *single* idea. Each sentence within the paragraph expresses a thought, and all these thoughts must be so closely related that they combine to develop one, and only one, idea.

Tagging a second idea onto the end of a paragraph results in a triple loss. Not only will that idea be submerged (when perhaps it ought to be given a paragraph of its own for full development), but the first idea, which is central to the paragraph, will suffer from the distracting influence of the second. Moreover, such paragraphs leave an impression of muddled thinking. The essence of a paragraph is unity.

The central idea of a paragraph is expressed in the topic sentence, which in business writing should ordinarily come first in the paragraph. Scanners and speed readers will find it easier to follow an argument if the most prominent position in the paragraph is occupied by the topic sentence. Other readers will also be helped, except when the need for a transition conflicts with the need to give the central thought first place. There is no entirely satisfactory way to resolve this conflict; the best that can be done is to start a paragraph with a transition sentence—or preferably a transition phrase, keeping it short—and to follow immediately with the topic sentence. Another helpful method is to underline (or italicize) topic sentences. In addition, free employment of headings and subheadings provides a visible outline for readers to follow.

The precise content of a topic sentence must be adapted to the method by which the paragraph in which it appears is developed. Logical development and illustration call for different kinds of topic sentences. For example, *In practice, authoritarian leaders run into difficulty* can open a paragraph that will cite specific problems dictatorial types encounter. But if the causes of difficulty are to be explored, then a better topic sentence might read, *Authoritarian leadership runs afoul of current trends, popular attitudes, and behavioral patterns*. If a paragraph will recite details, then the topic sentence should offer a generalization that unites them. A paragraph that follows a positive statement and enumerates the limits of its applicability should begin with a connective to help the reader change course; this is followed by a topic sentence that describes the purpose of the paragraph: *On the other hand, monetary rewards, as motivators, fall short in several respects*. By consciously selecting a development method and constructing a topic sentence in conformity with it, a business writer can proceed in a systematic, businesslike way, not at all dependent on anything as unreliable as inspiration. Furthermore, the writer's efforts will succeed in turning out an effective product, one that gets its message across.

On completing a paragraph, Harry Burns spends a minute reviewing it. Does the topic sentence succeed in tying it together? Are there any extraneous thoughts in the paragraph that don't relate closely enough to the topic sentence? Since the topic sentence must unify its paragraph, all extraneous thoughts probably need paragraphs of their own; although occasionally a topic sentence may be modified to encompass its entire paragraph as written. In any case, when a topic sentence and its paragraph are at odds, something remains to be done.

Balance

Among the methods of paragraph development discussed earlier was illustration. This method has much to recommend it, not all of the advantages being immediately obvious. In fact, illustration answers two kinds of problems that represent opposite extremes. Conceptual writing, unrelieved by concrete examples, appears to business readers like Ed Johnson as vague. In his view, such concentration on theoretical argument bespeaks an impractical mentality. Unable to relate conceptual statements to his own experience, and unwilling to go to the trouble of searching for details that might lend substance to the generalizations, Ed is likely to put down a theoretical argument as either unrealistic or irrelevant to his situation.

However, masses of facts can't be left to fall as they may, no matter how relevant the facts may be individually: such data must be accompanied by a generalization that binds them to one another. In the absence of such a synthesizing agent, business readers are likely to perceive only a chaotic jumble. Projecting his own bewilderment on the purveyor of these seemingly unrelated facts, Ed Johnson wonders about the confused state of mind that would produce such writing. Although presenting readers with recognizable facts and situations is necessary to understanding their meaning, it is far from sufficient. Wrapping up the package before delivery is obligatory.

Similarly, a bare repetition of the experience of a past period to show how a different set of decision criteria would have worked will not convince practical people; they will suspect that the proposed criteria were tailored to meet past—and not necessarily recurrent—situations. Some theoretical exposition should be incorporated in a practical demonstration.

To sum up, suitable development of a theme involves striking a balance between the general and the specific, by offering a combination of the two. When an argument comprises a string of generalizations, bring each generalization down to earth with concrete examples that are related to the experiences of the readers. Coming at the problem from the opposite direction, don't let your assortment of facts appear isolated from one another; gather them together under a covering umbrella—a topic sentence that generalizes about their common characteristics and their pertinence. Whether Harry Burns starts with a general statement and finds illustrations or begins with details and supplies a bond that holds them together, his finished product is recognizable as a unified paragraph developed according to the method of illustration.

Such a combination of the general and the specific avoids the misunderstandings that are bound to occur among readers who are not completely turned off—that is, among readers who earnestly try to follow what is being said. Unless guided properly with relevant details, many of these readers will apply the written generalizations to the wrong situations; and they will infer improper hypotheses from a recitation of facts, unless these are held together by appropriate general propositions. Accordingly, a general statement followed by illustrative detail is useful, not only in holding the interest of your readers, but also in keeping them on the right track as the argument moves ahead.

At the same time, maintaining a balance between the conceptual and the concrete protects Harry Burns from appearing either vague or confused, and also shields him from the blame that would inevitably come his way if his incomplete presentation allowed readers to drift into mistaken conclusions. Nor is such blame unjustified. A business writer who finds himself frequently misunderstood must assume a large measure of responsibility for having presented his material badly in the first place.

All sides of an argument

Appearances do count. A business writer must not appear confused, nor should he seem unduly negative. Yet these difficulties arise often among writers whose intent is merely to present both sides of a case fairly.

Perhaps it is deference to the opposition that leads some writers and speakers to accord too much prominence to negative views, or it is oversensitivity to the limitations of their own vantage point, or the cause is to be found among such traits as innate diffidence. In any case, audiences often suffer the discomfort of listening to a speaker who seems constantly to argue with himself by meticulously permitting reservations, contrary observations, partial retractions, exceptions, conditions, and refinements to interrupt his train of thought. A speech or a memorandum appears to battle against itself when it alternates between two views, with a multiplicity of *buts* and *howevers,* each reversing the one it follows. Going back and forth between the positive and the negative leaves the audience confused and weary.

A far better practice is to group all the positive statements and enunciate them together, followed by the negative comments, also grouped together and accurately labeled. The positive comes first, of course, to avoid creating a negative impression before the main points are established. So the order is one or more positive paragraphs, followed by one or more negative paragraphs. With limited material, a single paragraph can offer both the positive and negative sides, saying, in effect: *On the one hand . . . , whereas on the other hand.*

Another use of the negative is to tell what a thing is not—often a valuable part of a definition or a useful technique for delimiting the scope of a subject. Again, it is best to define the subject in positive terms first, before proceeding to the negative, saying: *This is what we are talking about; and that is excluded.*

Deliberate understatement

Polly Richardson has a better way to handle her own reluctance to go out on a limb: she simply avoids statements that are too definite or too strong. Even when sure of her ground, she shuns overstatement as a matter of course. Every statement she makes must be defensible—an overstatement is likely to wither embarrassingly under attack.

Deliberate understatement is not too extreme a protective device. Quite the contrary, it brings with it a set of advantages all its own. People who habitually understate their positions are not easily dislodged, counterattacked, or driven back to untenable defenses. Moderate statements forestall devastating attacks, and seldom lead to the embarrassment of a retreat.

An effective method for winning over an audience is to let an understated conclusion follow a particularly cogent argument. Reasoning that many readers will probably draw stronger conclusions of their own, Polly allows them that prerogative while underscoring the moderation of her own approach. Such a method partakes of the art of persuasion, which the ancients, in fact, linked to the science of logic.

Persuasion

Polly Richardson also uses other methods to persuade audiences. For example, having chosen to present a logical argument—with or without the negative side—and anxious to achieve a strong persuasive impact, she sometimes finds it useful to bring her readers to the point of expecting a conclusion and then letting them take that final step themselves. This method differs from simply offering readers an understated conclusion, and it is at least as effective.

Another variation is to offer alternatives and arguments, leaving readers to make the decision for themselves. This method provides advantages beyond that of subtly flattering an audience by showing respect for its ratiocinative powers. A reader who believes he has participated in arriving at a conclusion is likely to display greater tenacity in defending his position against opposing arguments. And if he thinks he made up his own mind, his conviction is likely to prove unshakable.

At first glance, this commentary may seem to conflict with a previous observation that an idea whose development is left vague or uncertain risks being stolen. Remember that we are now talking about persuasion, about gaining support and seeking action that will redound to your own credit. If you have to pass along the credit for an idea in order to see it executed, and if the result is to enhance your standing as a person who gets things done, then in most organizations you will have made a good bargain. In our society, the visible doers are rated higher than the profound thinkers. Consider *that* for a while.

In any case, a major mistake is to suppose that strong language makes an argument persuasive. Patently emotional appeals are held suspect, and exaggeration defeats itself. In dealing with intelligent people, understatement is much more effective than hyperbole.

Causal and casual relations

While profound thinkers are often denied the full measure of respect they might consider their due, shoddy thinkers are made to suffer for their carelessness. Surely everyone is aware that non sequiturs must be avoided and that unrelated items must not be thrown together as though they belonged to the same category in a proper classification scheme. Yet many business writers gratuitously assume that simultaneous occurrences are necessarily related to a common cause, or that the relation between an action and a subsequent condition *must* be causal, when in fact it may be only casual. In addition, causes are frequently mistaken for results, or mere symptoms are asserted as causes. All these logical fallacies impair the credibility of business writers.

The only safe course is to make no assumption as to causality unless adequate proof is in hand that the presumed system of causal factors is both necessary and sufficient to account for the results under study. Lacking such proof, marshal the facts without comment, propose a working hypothesis without claiming to have proved anything, or be content to suggest the possibility that hidden relations may exist.

Illustrations abound. Let a new management take over a company; it will often be unfairly held accountable for everything that happens, sometimes without even a grace period during which to make its influence felt. Long-range trends in the industry, long-term contracts still in force, new plants going into production after years of planning and construction, equipment suffering from years of neglect, and fluctuations in general economic conditions—all are brushed aside while a single factor, the change in management, is offered as explanation for every improvement or deterioration in results.

Those who deliberately seize on a simplistic approach often underrate the intelligence of their readers. Once an audience becomes aware of having been misled, the writer's deceptiveness is likely to create obstacles for him in the future. Accordingly, when your case rests on rigorous logic, review what you've written step by step to ascertain that each proposition is sufficient to justify the one that follows. Then go backward step by step to confirm that each proposition in turn is necessary to establish the one that follows it. Only when both conditions of necessity and sufficiency have been met can a conclusion be said to have been proved by rigorous logic. Only then can a business writer be satisfied with a presentation that purports to be logical.

Hedging

None of the legitimate methods cited above has anything in common with equivocation. Presenting all sides of a question can be a matter of fairness or a ploy to damp the impact of the other side's argument. Understatement can forestall embarrassment or appeal to readers who appreciate moderation. Permitting readers to draw their own conclusions can be a way to lure them to follow a lead voluntarily or a recognition of the inescapable fact that people, like horses, will drink the water only if they want to. In addition, caution in proclaiming cause-and-effect relations is a prudent course to follow. None of these methods demands weasel wording, ambiguity, or hedging. And none should make an audience uncomfortable.

The problem with hedging, as with other tactics for qualifying conclusions beyond the vanishing point, is that readers begin to suspect the motivation as well as the conclusions of the writer. They wonder about the facts, the thinking, and the methods. To discerning readers, the excesses that go by the name of hedging are not far removed from retraction. And if a business writer is going to withdraw his conclusions by sleight of hand, or decline responsibility for them, he would do better to refrain from offering them in the first place.

Paragraph length

How long should a paragraph be? The most sensible answer is a truism: A paragraph must be long enough to say what it has to say. A simple method of development, using limited material, tends to produce a short paragraph, whereas complex development requires a long paragraph. In addition, appropriate space allocation may dictate that a particular paragraph be cut back or enlarged. Sometimes consideration should be given to the medium: in writing for a magazine with narrow columns, remember that every paragraph will look longer than it is, whereas wide columns tend to give a short paragraph a skimpy appearance.

Clearly, arbitrary insistence on short paragraphs is indefensible. Length alone does not impair readability, nor does it detract from clarity of exposition. It is far better to explain a point carefully and completely than to leave readers dangling in midair merely to conform to a misguided criterion that no logic can support.

The short-short-short shibboleth advanced by advocates of short words, short sentences, and short paragraphs has been widely publicized, and perhaps widely accepted. Nevertheless, it is overrated and cannot be relied on as a guide to good business writing. With respect to paragraphs, a better set of guidelines is to open with the topic sentence, select a suitable method of development, and pursue it until the paragraph says fully what it is intended to say.

Summary

Each paragraph must carry out its function, which is to unfold a portion of the outline represented by a single caption. But that isn't all. The final test of a paragraph's efficacy lies in its appeal. To succeed in communicating its message, a paragraph must be audience-directed and readable.

After it has been written, a paragraph should be reviewed for a number of characteristics. It should develop a single idea, stated in a topic sentence at or near the beginning. It should use a limited number of compatible methods for development. In a word, it should hang together as a self-contained unit.

9 | *expressing a thought*

A thought is expressed by a sentence. One thought, one sentence. Several thoughts unfold an idea: several sentences, one paragraph.

Business writers are constantly importuned by exhortations to give their sentences readability, clarity, conciseness, and a host of other attributes. So far, so good; but observe how much of the advice turns sour as the advocates of mechanical criteria and unmitigated brevity monotonously churn out their short-short-short shibboleth. The preceding chapter noted that short paragraphs are not the best, and more is said about short words in a later chapter; it is time now for a good, hard look at sentences, and at the oft-repeated admonition to be brief and simple (presumably, make your writing simple).

Does arithmetic help?

The latter-day adherents of brevity have strayed so far from the original theory that they are advocating a parody or a perversion of the concept that the *average* length of sentences people can tolerate varies with their education. There is no quarrel with that concept; the elaborations on it are something else. True, there was a time, some centuries ago, when mastery of the language was demonstrated by flaunting an ability to handle extremely long and involved sentences. Perhaps the readers of those days derived a sense of achievement from their arduous efforts at comprehension. But it is also true that even the longest of such sentences can be broken down into many smaller ones, if sentences come to be defined so that they may end with colons or semicolons as well as periods—one of the refinements introduced by the mini-unit writing school. But then the stylists of earlier days punctuated their long sentences with tiny ones, so that on average they weren't far removed from today's practicality after all.

The real questions now are these: first, whether *every* sentence has to be, or ought to be, short; and second, whether arithmetical calculations improve a piece of writing. To ask these questions is virtually to answer them. An unrelieved succession of short sentences can only drive readers away. If the childishness doesn't offend them, the monotony will put them to sleep. A speaker of course has more freedom than a writer: he can select words or passages for emphasis, inject variety into his delivery, and run short sentences together—or split up long ones—as he delivers them. Furthermore, he can and should use short sentences much more freely than a writer. Nevertheless, the staccato effect of an unbroken string of short sentences is deadening.

As for calculations that determine the number of words in an average sentence, or the number of syllables in an average word, they remind one of actress Gina Lollobrigida's response to a reporter's question concerning her physical measurements: "Why do you need numbers," she said, "when you can see with your eyes?" A similar question applies to writing by arithmetical formulas: "Why should anyone need numbers when he can listen with his ears?"

Yet the cult of shortness thrives, and the reason is not

hard to find: shortness does incidentally stumble on a way to avert certain real problems. But since the problems do exist, and since mere shortness does not make good business writing, effective solutions to actual problems must be adopted. Once the problems are known, just that awareness is an excellent defensive weapon in the business writer's hands.

The first rule in composing a sentence is to stick to a single thought. If the thought is simple, the sentence should also be simple. Running two thoughts into the same sentence threatens to make both thoughts obscure. However, no succession of simple sentences will serve to explain a complex relation nearly as well as a single complex sentence. There it is: *A sentence must be designed to accommodate the thought it presents—a simple sentence for a simple thought, and a complex sentence for a complex thought. Only the introduction of fruitless complications is wrong.*

The second problem in constructing sentences has to do with heaviness: a succession of ponderous sentences can become quite tedious. But if sentences must be long—that is to say, if they convey complex thoughts—then the solution lies not in chopping them up, thoughts and all, but in separating them with short sentences that relieve the tedium. That's easy to do. And it works.

A third problem made worse by interminably long sentences is bombast. Surely a reader finds it painful to wade through wordy, pompous pronouncements; for a business writer the solution is to cultivate a regard for his readers. Pomposity is a form of foolishness that can be avoided without tricks—for instance, the trick of shortening all sentences. All that is required is thoughtfulness and an audience-directed approach.

Fourth among the problems aggravated by the length of sentences is the physical separation of words in ways that confuse readers. Because verbs are closely related to their subjects, good business writing requires that subject and verb be physically close within a sentence. Take the following example of a poorly constructed sentence: *A meeting of the department heads, chaired by the divisional vice-president for operations, after hearing all the arguments and rebuttals of the parties to the dispute and discussing the merits of the case on both sides, rendered its decision in favor of.* . . . By the time Ed Johnson gets to the verb *rendered*, he has forgotten that the subject is *meeting*.

Similarly, relative pronouns *(he, she, it, they, his, her, their, who, whose, that, which)* must be physically close to the antecedent nouns they stand for. Indeed, long sentences create situations in which a business writer may be tempted to separate a relative pronoun from its antecedent (more will be said on this subject later) or a verb from its subject; however, since sheer length is not the problem here, careful writing can do more for the reader than is possible merely by conforming to a rule that demands that all sentences be short. Two effective methods for overcoming problems with relative pronouns are to restructure sentences and to repeat nouns, where necessary. In this instance, restructuring involves nothing more than rearranging words so that antecedent noun and relative pronoun occupy adjacent positions. If that solution is not possible, then the relative pronoun should be discarded and the antecedent noun repeated.

In short, any thought—complex or simple—suffers from having useless embellishments, distracting irrelevancies, redundant material, or additional thoughts tacked onto it. Nevertheless, a truly complex thought needs to be expressed in a complex sentence. Such a thought can be destroyed otherwise. Problems that are exacerbated—but not caused—by the lengths of sentences should be addressed directly, and not circumvented by such dubious methods as chopping up the sentences irrationally.

Directness

Another frequently heard admonition is to write "direct" sentences, apparently a vague reference to the indicative mood (plain, declarative statements)—as though all other moods must be driven out of business writing. Actually, each mood and voice has its place; and while the indicative mood does predominate, it is not the only string on the business writer's instrument.

As illustration, take the imperative mood (commands). It is the most effective method for writing procedures. Compare these three versions of an instruction:

◇ *Invoice, purchase order, and receiving slip are compared by the accounts payable clerk. If these documents are in agreement and all prior approvals are in order, a voucher is prepared for payment.*

◇ *The accounts payable clerk compares invoice, purchase order, and receiving slip. If these documents are in agreement, and prior approvals are in order, he prepares a voucher for payment.*

◇ *Accounts payable clerk: Compare invoice, purchase order, and receiving slip. If these documents are in agreement and all prior approvals are in order, prepare a voucher for payment.*

The last version, written in recipe style (the imperative mood), is the least irksome, especially when a person must read a great many instructions to comprehend a single procedure. Incidentally, a command is about as *direct* as a statement can get.

Do questions have a place in business writing? Of course they do—and not only in documents headed "Questionnaire." Although writing that is studded with too many questions can become tiresome, occasional use of the interrogatory mood introduces variety and can produce a desirable effect: it may get readers to stop and think about their answers.

The subjunctive mood also has its uses, especially when the writing is about something that has not happened or may not happen. *If this legislation had been enacted, then the industry would now be required to meet certain new standards.* Again, *If a snowstorm should delay deliveries of raw materials, our inventories would meet production demands for two weeks.* In practice, the subjunctive *would* and *should* are encountered less frequently in modern business writing than elsewhere. They are in fact avoided whenever the indicative can carry the meaning as well. But the subjunctive is not always avoidable, as the previous examples demonstrate.

The mood of a sentence is carried by its verb—if it has one. Although going verbless may be frowned on by some as "bad grammar," the practice has always held an honorable place in the standard language. Indeed, it can be most effective in punctuating remarks. Or as an eye-catcher. What, after all, is wrong with *So far, so good* as a sentence? Why not put *For a while, at least* between two periods, for effect? Or the expression, *Especially in the present circumstances*—surely it does the job efficiently. Or, *Not that everything fell into place automatically. Indeed not.* Additionally, in modern business writing, a clause is often split away to form a verbless sentence standing by itself. Instead of tacking *which means that* . . . onto the end of a sentence, the writer begins a new sentence——*Meaning:* . . . . Other words used similarly to quicken the pace are *Caution:* . . . , *Recommended:* . . . , *Example:* . . . . When not overdone, the method unquestionably lends punch to business writing.

Besides mood, a verb carries the voice of a sentence, which may be either active or passive. For example, a clerk did things (active voice) or things were done by a clerk (passive voice). On repetition, the passive voice tends to become tiresome and should therefore be avoided. Often a switch to the active voice can be accomplished by changing the point of view: instead of *being faced with problems,* a person may *face problems*. Even inanimate objects can be active subjects: *an axle squeaks*—and then it is heard.

The passive voice can also be used occasionally to give a prominent position to the thing acted upon, because of its overriding importance, or because it is to become the subject of the section being introduced. Example: *The President was escorted by secret service agents.* The sheer novelty of a passive sentence breaking into a chain of active sentences lends significance to whatever it says. And that's another reason to use it sparingly.

Inversion

The conversion of a sentence from active to passive involves shuffling of words. Instead of *A did B to C*, we say *B was done to C by A*. Another change in word order is effected by a question, which puts the verb before the subject. Thus: *Did A do B to C?* or *Was B done to C by A?* Actually, inversion of the word order can be accomplished within the indicative mood, without asking a question: *B was what A did to C*. Or, instead of *A answered so*, it is permissible (but strange) to write *Thus did A answer*—producing a new emphasis. A change in word order is called for when it clarifies the meaning, as in this illustration:

Original: *Buy the assets from the parent corporation rather than its stock.*

Revised: *Buy from the parent corporation its assets rather than its stock.*

Alternative revision: *Buy the parent corporation's assets rather than its stock.*

For emphasis, a phrase like *under the circumstances* can be placed at the beginning of a sentence. At other times the same phrase might be allowed to dangle at the end, or even be lost in the middle. The placement of words can augment their impact or improve the readability of the sentence; the choice should of course always be made consciously. In the next example, a change in word order, for emphasis, is accompanied by a switch from adjective to adverb.

Original: *The board has issued a definitive statement reading. . . .*

Revised: *Definitively, the board's statement reads. . . .*

Perhaps most important of all, clauses can be reversed; this is frequently done to bring a relative pronoun closer to its antecedent. This problem of proximity is among the most perplexing in business writing, yet it need not be. The rule is simply that a relative pronoun must never be far removed from its antecedent noun, because any other noun standing between the two may create ambiguity for the reader. A few examples will clarify this point.

Original: *They will look for reactions by the defense which will help them appraise the strength of the case.*
Revised: *They will look for defense reactions which will help them appraise the strength of the case.*
Original: *The project will be undertaken in stages, the first of which requires that the systems department prepare a written procedure. It then progresses to. . . .*

If *it* refers to the procedure, there is no problem. But if the pronoun refers to the project, then the intervening nouns *department* and *procedure* do confuse things. A change in the structure of one of the sentences can often bring an antecedent noun closer to its relative pronoun. That is,

Revised: *The systems department prepares a written procedure in the first stage of the project, which then progresses to. . . .*

If switching clauses doesn't work, and a pronoun can't be brought close to its antecedent, it's better to repeat the noun than to allow the confusion to stand. Such repetition is not really objectionable, despite the widespread fear that grips business writers on these occasions and causes them to elect an inferior course without so much as considering the alternative. Audiences tolerate repetition quite well. Besides, the technique of using synonyms to avoid repetition is not as safe as it may appear. When a business writer speaks first of a *computer,* then of a *central processing unit,* and finally of a *black box* (all the while referring to the same piece of equipment), a segment of his audience will look for—and probably devise—subtle distinctions that were never intended. Repetition is preferable to straining for synonyms—what Fowler called "elegant variation."

A common fault of business writing is the use of a relative pronoun without an antecedent at all. Whether the writer has lost track of what he was saying or the intended antecedent is several sentences back, a reader has no way of discovering. He is lost without a compass. A relative pronoun must have an antecedent noun to which it refers. Moreover, the relative pronoun should literally *follow* its antecedent in virtually all circumstances. A relative pronoun that precedes its "antecedent" can be disconcerting to readers. A possible exception occurs when a relative pronoun is not really needed, and it serves merely to replace an article. For example, *From its inception, the program was well received.* In this case, the words *from its inception* could easily be replaced by *from the beginning.*

For reasons of emphasis, coherence, or logical development, the expression of a thought can often be improved by the simple expedient of rearranging the sequence of words or clauses. Although not a cure-all for whatever is wrong, this method can offer considerable help to the perplexed business writer. He has not made a total effort to get his message across until he has played with word order, trying one way and then another to bring his meaning out with greater clarity.

Some inversions of normal word order are best avoided as mere affectations. For example, *in so doing* is not as straightforward as *in doing so.* Also the positioning of adverbs after the verbs they modify is generally more natural than reversing the order.

Clarity

Since clarity is essential to effective communication, those who feel compelled to issue pronouncements to business writers frequently declare that writing must have clarity, but they rarely offer any hint as to how that admonition is to be heeded. Actually, clarity may mean one of two things—readability or precision. It depends on the writer's purpose.

Many circumstances require a degree of precision that defeats readability. For example, written procedures to instruct people at many locations in conforming with a uniform system, regulations promulgated for consistent enforcement of a law, and documents to bind people in the performance of specified duties or the avoidance of specified acts—these all have a number of characteristics in common. They must include considerable detail; they must spell out what is or is not to be done in situations that may be anticipated; they must describe exceptions, limitations, and variations. It may be taken as axiomatic that any piece of writing that meets these needs cannot also be readable.

Hence the trade-off between readability and precision: the greater the need for precision, the less chance that readable prose will come out of the writing effort. Nevertheless, it is always necessary to work over heavy writing and make it as readable as possible without sacrificing *necessary* precision. And when extremes of precision are not mandatory—as in situations where guides can safely replace rules, or when the intention is to familiarize people with something new rather than provide them with a standing reference—a good business writer will prefer to forgo excessive refinement of his remarks in the interests of communicating in a style that is more likely to hold reader attention and to get the essential message across.

When addressing two audiences simultaneously, a business writer can reach both, not by making a compromise between readability and precision—for such a compromise is unworkable—but by offering separate material to those who need instructions and to those who require only a general description of content. Thus a letter of transmittal may accompany a procedure, a précis may summarize a technical report, or a preamble may describe and outline a regulation. In each case, the short, general version must be made readable if it is to accomplish its objective.

A more difficult method makes use of two kinds of type: descriptive, readable passages are printed in standard type, whereas precise, detailed material that documents the argument point by point appears in reduced type, perhaps indented for further differentiation.

Ponderous writing is not the only enemy of clarity. A frequent mistake among business writers is abuse of ellipsis: leaving out words that are required to make the meaning clear. To illustrate, *Branch managers have been instructed to personally inspect inventories on hand and will report obsolete items to the controller.* The subject of the verb *will report* is obscure, because a pronoun has been elided. Inserting a *they* would help. Alternatively, the sentence can be cleaned up and restructured: *After inspecting inventories, as instructed, branch managers will report obsolete items to the controller.*

Parallelism

Once the reader's mind set has been established, it must be respected. Consider the difficulty of mentally adding twelve thousand five hundred to thirty-four hundred, compared with the ease of adding twelve thousand five hundred and three thousand four hundred. The first addition requires an adjustment, because of the inconsistency in presenting the numbers. Likewise, in working with written numbers, binary 101001 plus decimal 35 is much more difficult to cope with than 41 plus 35, where both numbers are expressed in the decimal mode.

In business writing, too, when several thoughts are held up for comparison, it is helpful to frame them in a consistent pattern. This uniformity, or parallelism, is useful not only in making comparisons but also in constructing tabulations and enumerations of alternatives or associated items.

Parallelism may take a number of forms, which may be illustrated most dramatically in lists. A list of reasons for investing personal funds might read:

To augment income immediately
To accumulate capital for retirement
To prepare to finance a specific project
To establish a fund for emergencies

Contrast the neatness of such a presentation with the following list of benefits derivable from formal education:

Higher earnings over one's working life
To be able to relate current events to the past
Acquiring knowledge in specific fields
Familiarity with the cultural side of life
To grasp the significance of the human experience

Obviously, an enumeration gains attractiveness when its elements are alike: all infinitives, all participial phrases, all phrases dependent on nouns, or all full sentences. When complete sentences are employed, their verbs should be in the same form, including tense, mood, and voice.

For most purposes, it is sufficient to limit parallelism to the first few words, or to carry it to the general form in which each element is put. But sometimes complete parallelism, down to details, enhances the effectiveness of a comparison. Consistency in detail may extend to the number of phrases in each parallel sentence; the number of modifiers preceding each noun or verb; the presence or absence of the articles *a, an,* and *the;* or the rhythm patterns of components. In general, the closer the correspondence between the items in a list, the sentences in a paragraph, or the parts of a sentence, the more likely that careful readers will compare them with each other.

However, there is another side to parallelism. If two clauses or sentences are not intended for comparison, then it is better to give them different structures. An alteration of any sort is preferable to a parallelism that invokes spurious comparisons. Writing parallel sentences is fairly easy; making nonparallel sentences is easier still. All that is required of a writer is consciousness of the parallel concept and a small effort to hold his readers on the track.

To illustrate with a simple example: *The previous system suffered from delays in posting transactions and coding errors.* On a quick reading, the parallel between two participles—*posting* and *coding*—makes it appear that errors were being coded (just as transactions were being posted) and that the coding process had suffered delay. It would be better to avoid a spurious parallelism in this situation by saying *delays in posting and errors in coding*. The parallel now is useful. It helps the reader to grasp the meaning quickly.

Related to parallelism in purpose, though different in method, is the use of an apposite word combination to emphasize a relation between the parts of a sentence. *If . . . , then . . .* is particularly helpful when there is more than one condition. Thus: *If . . . , and if . . . , then. . . .* The combination *not only . . . , but also . . .* may take several forms: *not merely . . . , but . . . in addition; not solely . . . , but . . . as well.* Although *either . . . or* is found fairly often, *neither . . . nor* is seldom seen. Despite familiarity with these standard combinations, business writers unaccountably neglect most of them. To improve the clarity of your writing, make constant use of these devices.

The combination *on the one hand . . . ; on the other hand . . .* is especially valuable in preventing ambiguity when there is more than one statement on either hand, or more than one element. Take this simple example: *Comparisons between men and women and bulls and cows are specious at best.* Now see what happens when a few words are inserted: *Comparisons between men and women, on the one hand, and bulls and cows, on the other hand, are specious at best.*

Punctuating a sentence

By one definition, a sentence is whatever appears between two periods. Business writers tend to worry too much about the punctuation that separates words, phrases, and clauses within a sentence—only to give up in despair. A little thought will accomplish more than a lot of worry.

The long-term trend in writing of all kinds is toward less punctuation. The tendency is to help readers move along quickly. Unnecessary impediments are dispensed with, including a great many commas routinely inserted in an earlier time. In modern business writing, commas are used to help the reader comprehend words in groups. For example, a parenthetic expression, inserted anywhere in a sentence, is generally separated by commas instead of parentheses. This device involves *two* commas, unless the parenthetic expression begins or ends a sentence.

When modifiers are related, as in *dark blue ornament,* commas between the modifiers are eliminated. A hyphen may be used when two words act in unison to modify another, as in *fast-moving organization, machine-sensible data,* and *punched-card equipment.* But if no ambiguity results from omitting a hyphen, standard usage condones doing without, especially in the predicate: *The equipment accepts punched cards.*

Some types of word combinations should be joined by slashes (virgules) instead of hyphens. Thus, when a ratio is implied, as in comparing costs and benefits, it seems natural to prefer the slash: *cost/benefit, debt/equity, price/earnings* all involve ratios. Alternatives also are commonly joined by slashes: *yes/no condition, input/output equipment, go/no-go gauge.* However, one common abuse of the virgule should be avoided: *and/or* is awkward and unnecessary; *or* alone carries the same sense.

When too many commas lead to obscurity, semicolons may help to clarify a sentence. In these situations, semicolons separate the major word groups, while commas separate words within the major groups. To illustrate: *Customers are classified as domestic, Western Hemisphere, or overseas; industrial, wholesale, or retail; and cash, credit card, or house account.*

Semicolons are helpful also in juxtaposing closely related thoughts. Sometimes each of two thoughts is so much a part of a single idea that they are best expressed jointly in a single sentence with a semicolon between them. Whereas two clauses separated by a comma require a connective, a semicolon can stand without one. Unfortunately, semicolons are seldom encountered in business writing, probably because of an irrational fear of them on the part of business writers. However, while semicolons may appear strange to a person in the act of writing, they cause no uneasiness to the person reading. Hence, business writers can afford to be much bolder in using semicolons. Readers would not be offended, and business writing would improve.

The colon also could be used to greater advantage. Business writers customarily use colons to precede enumerations. Nothing wrong there. But often a colon can replace a *for example*, an *i.e.*, or an *e.g.*—and few literary devices deserve to be replaced more than those abbreviations. In addition, a colon can link a conceptual statement and a concrete illustration: facts to support an abstract proposition.

Quotation marks are frequently misused in business writing. They should set off direct quotations, of course; but they cannot relieve an author of responsibility for his own selection of words. The writer who is embarrassed by slang, jargon, or clichés should avoid them. If he must use them, then unabashed delivery is better than highlighting or apologizing with quotation marks.

When quotation marks are necessary, the placement of the closing mark can be perplexing. It always follows a comma or period, whereas it precedes a colon or semicolon. When a quotation ends in a question, the closing quotation mark follows the other punctuation, but if a question is not raised by the quotation itself, then the quotation mark precedes the question mark. A few illustrations: *The group asked for a speaker who would "tell it straight." The group asked, "Will he tell it straight?" If a released convict may be said to have "paid his debt to society," can a pardoned criminal be said to have, in some way, "paid his dues to society"?*

The rule for parentheses is simpler. If a full sentence is included within parentheses, then the other punctuation—period, question mark, exclamation point—precedes the final parenthesis. Otherwise, the other punctuation goes outside the parenthesis and this rule holds for periods as well as question marks (contrary to the rule for quotations).

The trend toward simplicity has also affected the rules

pertaining to capitalization. Titles and departments need not be capitalized: *purchasing agent* and *purchasing department* look right in lowercase. Moreover, references to *the* or *a department* should never be capitalized. Business people are accustomed to working with numbers and seeing them in print. It is unnecessary to spell them out. Yet, in dealing with two sets of numbers simultaneously, a purpose is served in spelling out one set. For example: *Ten percent of items accounted for 50% of sales, and thirty percent of items for 70% of sales.*

Obviously, a sentence should never end with a number that incorporates a decimal. The appearance of two periods creates ambiguity when a sentence reads, *The constant was calculated to be 25.906.* Likewise, confusion results from *The unit price is $2.750.* The solution lies in restructuring the sentence, adding words or inserting a semicolon followed by a second clause. Altering the previous illustrations: *A constant of 25.906 was derived by calculations. The price is $2.750 per piece.*

Before going to press, magazines and books are gone over thoroughly by copyeditors, who clean up errors in punctuation. Provided, of course, that the copyeditors can decipher the author's meaning. Business writers would do better to cooperate with their copyeditors and their secretaries by punctuating their manuscripts properly themselves. And if attention to commas, semicolons, and colons leads business writers to more imaginative use of these marks, so much the better. However, a poorly constructed sentence cannot be salvaged by punctuation. It will have to be rewritten.

IV | to do it better

10 | *the way it's said*

It should come as no surprise to anyone that people communicate the way they think. Thinking is not always logical, and neither is communication. Languages characteristically develop from a logical base that can be defined by rules of grammar, building thereon accumulated overlays of habits and customs that defy categorization and determine usage. To take a simple example of logical inconsistency in idiomatic usage, note that *helped prepare* is accepted usage, whereas *assisted prepare* is not (some business writing notwithstanding). As another illustration, one may either *ask a person to do something* or *ask that he do it*, but one cannot *request a person to do something;* one *requests that the other person do it.* When usage and grammar conflict, usage always predominates.

The preeminence of usage

Because of these unpredictable linguistic practices, a sizable number of enigmas in language confound logic and "grammatical rules." One example, the verbless sentence, has already been noted. As another illustration, *who* is used regularly where strict grammar clearly calls for *whom*. Indeed, the use of *whom* is common now only when preceded by a preposition: *to whom, for whom, with whom, by whom*. *Whose* can have an inanimate antecedent: *a system whose purpose is sound deserves careful planning and implementation*. It is unnecessarily cumbersome to avoid *whose* by saying *the purpose of which*. *That* can replace *who* in referring to people. (But to achieve a lean style, try deleting both *that* and *who* wherever possible.)

Will has all but replaced *shall*, despite efforts to preserve distinctions between them. Also, sentences can properly begin with *And* or *But;* and they can properly end on prepositions like *on, in,* and *at. None*—although it means no one—can take a plural verb as easily as a singular: *None of the members were (or was) present*. And infinitives can be split: *to absolutely forbid* split infinitives would make many sentences awkward. Not all of the foregoing examples of usage are illogical; some defy purist "rules" that were mere inventions in the first place. The rules themselves were never accepted widely; that's all.

A good basic guide seems to be that a proposed grammatical rule that creates awkwardness will ultimately be broken often enough to force acceptance of usage that runs counter to the rule. Awkwardness is the real enemy of communication. Hence, business writers are well advised to replace purist prejudices with a concept of grace, a concept that can be developed by reading those writers who display commendable style. Only one proviso need be added: The expectations of readers must be respected to some extent. If a group unquestioningly accepts a supposed rule as valid, then it is risky to flout that judgment, poor though it may be. Thus, the business writer who finds himself among people who look with horror on *And* at the beginning of a paragraph is well advised to start his paragraphs some other way.

To sum up, although logic controls the organizing of material, the structuring of manuscripts, and the planning of paragraphs, it bows to standard usage wherever a conflict develops. Logic is not to be discarded altogether, but is rather to be regarded as an uncertain guide.

There is danger in carrying these observations too far. An anything-goes school appears to argue that whatever device succeeds in giving a reader comprehension of the text is acceptable as a way of communicating messages. Adherents of this doctrine contend that there are no fixed laws, and change is the order of the day——every day. Extremists even reject dictionaries for failing to convey the "true" meanings of words.

Fortunately for those who are serious in their desire to communicate, few people are sufficiently tolerant of bad grammar and bad usage to say, "As long as readers understand, it's OK." Actually, accepted usage changes very slowly. People are quite conservative about their habits of speech. To be sure, fads come and go, leaving no lasting mark; but even the most permissive authorities don't revise their thinking to accommodate such transitory phenomena. And when dictionaries are cast aside, where does one look for definitions of words? Surely some form of guide is necessary.

Before a writer decides to formulate his own rules, hopefully maintaining that his readers will understand him, he had better reexamine his premises. Reasonable assurance of understanding between writer and reader requires prior agreement as to standards. Authorities hesitate to claim correctness for their views—perhaps some confusion stems from this cause—but *standard usage* is an unobjectionable term for describing the body of thinking to which business writers ought to adhere.

The place of grammar

Since standard usage is superimposed on a grammatical—which is to say, a logical—foundation, the true rules of grammar must not be flouted. A few such rules will be discussed here because they are the cause of much confusion among business and technical writers.

Verbs indicate *tense*, which requires adherence to logic. No one has any difficulty in sorting out future, present, and past happenings; but it should be noted that the present tense is often used in describing future action or in telling a story that involves past action. It is often more convenient to write in the present tense, and there is nothing wrong with that practice. The present tense should also be used for concepts of universal, timeless application, even in the midst of a narrative written in the past tense. Also, if some acts precede others, it is proper to make time distinctions, even within sentences, rather than preserve a single tense throughout. While writing in the present, one shifts to the past when necessary. Likewise, *an event that occurred in the past could have been caused by acts that had taken place earlier*. The past perfect is necessary to make such time distinctions. Similarly, there are occasions when it is anticipated that *one act will have been completed and another act will then be undertaken*.

To sum up, most business writing should be in the present tense. All contemporaneous events agree as to tense, whereas prior or subsequent events should be indicated by changes in tense. But even though the pattern must follow a consistent logic, that does not mean that a single tense must be used throughout a piece of writing, or even that an entire paragraph or sentence must be confined to a single tense.

Another source of trouble in business writing is *number:* the agreement between noun and verb as to singularity or plurality. A singular noun must, of course, be accompanied by a singular verb. Yet four questions arise, as the following illustrations demonstrate.

◇ *One dime or two nickels are required for the meter to operate*. Here a compound subject has both a singular and a plural component. Proximity to the verb controls: the number of the verb is governed by the nearest component of the subject. However, deliberately placing the plural component next to the verb generally makes the reading smoother.

◇ *A committee deliberates; the committee members deliberate.* In American business usage, collective nouns take singular verbs. If a plural verb is wanted, perhaps in order to point up diversity within a group, then a word like *members* should be inserted.

◇ *A series of breakdowns was responsible for lowering production.* The subject is *series*, which is singular, and not *breakdowns.* Of course, the problem could have been avoided by saying, *A series of breakdowns lowered production.* Number problems are frequently amenable to such avoidance by turning to a verb without number, ordinarily in the past or future tense.

◇ *The base is the total of tax preference and. . . .* The writer who leaves out that *of* is creating a number problem for himself.

Many number problems arise in business writing when subject and verb are separated by intervening clauses, and the writer falls victim to the confusion he has himself created. The solution lies not in abandoning long sentences, as some might argue, but rather in keeping verbs in close proximity to their subjects.

Negatives pose problems of their own, especially when sentences become involved. *No one who has not* can only lead to complications that are avoidable with *anyone who has.* Again, a *no* automatically covers all the nouns in a sequence. If only one negative is intended, then that one should be segregated from the other nouns. Similarly with verbs and adjectives: *not absent and available* is confusing, because it says *neither absent nor available,* probably without intending to say that. By contrast, the positive *present and available* is clear. Here are examples of a kind of business writing that is seen too often:

◇ *Our bank cannot recommend a convertible issue to our clients unless their shares are not undervalued.*

◇ *Disclosure is not required of a loss contingency involving an unassisted claim or assessment when there has been*

*no manifestation by a potential claimant of an awareness
of a possible claim or assessment unless it is considered
probable that a claim will be asserted and there is a reasonable possibility that the outcome will be unfavorable.*

◊ *The corporation will not lose its Subchapter S status
unless the increase in stockholders occurs within five years,
except where the new stockholders inherited their holdings.*

The piling up of *not, unless,* and *except* is too much to
ask readers to follow. Even worse, writers with a predilec-
tion for negative construction—forgetting that they started
with a negative—often go on to contradict their own statement in the latter part of a long sentence. The most ludicrous lapses arise when double negatives and triple negatives
creep in unnoticed to destroy all semblance of logic. Words
to beware include *unless, except,* and *without.*

The best business writing avoids negatives for the most
part. This avoidance is intended not only to obviate problems but also to emphasize a positive tone. It is the doers,
not the naysayers, who dominate business organizations; it
is a positive outlook that gets the best reception. So on all
counts—orientation toward the audience, projection of a
good image, and clarity of expression—positive writing is
best.

As in many grammatical matters, a dangling word or
phrase is more easily illustrated than explained. In the
sentence, *Coming to the point, the operation has been a
disaster,* the participle *coming* dangles. One may ask: So
what? It's a good question. Such danglers don't really trouble a reader. But other danglers cause confusion: *Having
corrected the errors, the computer accepts the new input
for processing.* The participle *having corrected* attaches to
the nearest noun; in this sentence, a computer is said to
have corrected errors—and that may conceivably be true.
However, if the errors are corrected by people, and the
computer then accepts corrected input, the sentence is
misleading.

A dangling phrase at the end damages this sentence: *The
auditor should be aware of his responsibility should his*

judgment prove incorrect with the benefit of hindsight. What is meant is: *The auditor will be held responsible should subsequent developments prove his judgment incorrect.*

A particularly glaring type of grammatical error is so easy to detect that it ought never to slip by unnoticed. It is caused by intervening words that lead a writer to lose sight of relations and to slide into solecisms involving disagreement in one form or another. The solution is to test multiple constructions by elision of the in-between words. For example, *has and will follow the pattern* proves immediately to be faulty when read *has . . . follow the pattern.*

The lean style

After usage and grammar, style is the next important ingredient to master in achieving readable business writing. The style to strive for is *lean,* which means stripped of all unnecessary words. Business writing should be economical, with every word carrying its own weight; *Every word must contribute to conveying a message, clarifying a point, or enhancing readability.*

A suitable, businesslike style can be illustrated by enumerating sources of excess verbiage to eliminate:

◇   First, superfluous words occur so frequently that the simple expedient of questioning the need for each word can produce marvelous results. *Sales have been at near the record levels of last year* becomes *Sales were near last year's record levels.* From the same corporate report, *Demand for the product, however, is weak at the present time, but is improving* can be rewritten as *Present demand for the product is weak, but improving.* No words have been changed, and clarity has been enhanced by a reduction of 35 percent in verbiage. *They are inclined to accept the first proposal* is correct; nevertheless, *They incline toward the first proposal* is better. An action verb replaces a verb of being, to good effect. *What kind of numbers are we talking about?* illustrates a frequently encountered misuse of the word *kind* to create verbiage. *Kind* should not be made to stand for *size;* and the *size of numbers* is only an awkward reference to *quantities* or *volumes.* Better say, *What quantities are we talking about?*

Superfluities dealing with time seem to be popular: *Additional bulletins will be issued from time to time in the future*—as though readers might otherwise wait for bulletins to be issued in the past. The other way around, readers have been informed that a particular *forecast is based on a review of past history*—implying perhaps that others might attempt to review future history. Delays are specified to be *time delays,* despite the fact that there can be no other kind.

◇   Second, the glaring redundancy called pleonasm is so commonplace in business writing that people seem to mistake it for standard usage. *When, as, and if each and every man and woman achieves and attains his or her aims and goals totally and completely, then and only then will departmental and divisional budgets and profit plans be met and surpassed to the satisfaction and gratification of management and stockholders*—this indeed sounds very much like the writing people in business are exposed to daily. The sentence says no more than, *When all persons attain their goals, departmental budgets will be met*—a sentiment not worth all the fuss. A merciful author cleanses his writing of pleonasms for the sake of his audience.

◇   Third, modifiers that contribute nothing to the sense are a prime source of turgidity. In business and technical writing, adjectives and adverbs that tell readers something they need to know certainly have a place. For instance, it is often necessary to refer to a *blue* copy or a *flat* surface. However, mere description for its own sake is unwanted; and habitual use of nonessential words can turn crisp language soggy, when it doesn't actually engender bombast.

People in business write about *practical* experience, as though there might be some other kind. They tell their readers to establish *necessary* criteria, when it is inconceivable that anyone would want to establish *unnecessary* criteria. If the opposite of a modifier makes no sense at all, then the modifier itself can't be saying much. So why use it?

Even useful modifiers can often be dispensed with by selecting more precise nouns or verbs. A substance can be said to *produce an explosive reaction, produce an explosion, react explosively,* or *explode.* The primary consideration is to express the meaning, including nuances, precisely. The next most important factor is simplicity.

A business writer can forestall excessive use of modifiers by habitually selecting precise verbs. Even simple verbs should be chosen with care. For example, *having* an advantage is not the same as *gaining* an advantage; and *seizing* an advantage is something else again. It is just such distinctions that separate writers from nonwriters of business copy. Likewise, it is unlikely that a reception just happened to *take place.* Perhaps the planner deserves some credit for having brought off an event.

Some modifiers become attached to words and are carelessly brought in whether they serve a useful purpose or not. For a while, every risk became a *calculated risk,* even when there was no possibility of making a calculation. It is doubtful also that every *considered opinion* has really received all that consideration. Perhaps people are afraid to venture opinions or take risks without implying that they have given these matters deep thought. In an extreme case, a writer had this to say: *It is rather hazardous to attempt to predict. . . . However, I am going to stick my neck out and. . . .* A prediction may be *made,* or perhaps *hazarded,* flatly. There is nothing to be gained from *attempting to predict.*

Especially annoying are intensives like *very, highly, greatly, extremely,* because they frequently compound a bad situation and lean toward overstatement—whereas understatement, or at least moderation, is the technique to cultivate. After all, emphasis can only be relative. It is impossible to stress everything, and excessive use of superlatives must end by detracting from the whole. It is surprising how many business writers find ordinary things to be *extremely ordinary.* Another popular absurdity is *most unique:* would anyone say *most one-of-a-kind?* As an exercise in discipline, try removing all intensives from your vocabulary for a while. When tempted to write *moving very fast,* look for a synonym—like *speeding*—and then ask "Is this what I mean?" The exercise will be rewarding.

The practice of converting a verb to an adjective (requiring another verb in combination) leads to weak and wordy writing. It is better that an example *illustrate* than *be illustrative of;* it is better to *report* than to *submit a report;* and it is better to *write* than to *communicate in writing.* Even useful adjective-noun or adverb-verb combinations can often be replaced advantageously by specific nouns or verbs: to *move slowly* may be to *dawdle, delay, stall,* or *crawl.* Such substitutions enliven a piece of writing, and they may also add precision.

A straightforward style is essential to good business writing. A dangerous practice is the gratuitous addition of words that may lead a reader to infer a meaning the writer does not intend. For example, casually adding *at this time* invites a reader to suppose that a different conclusion might have been drawn at other times. The more careless business writers often toss contradictory words into the same sentence, and a reader is left to wonder why the writer said *always* at first, only to modify his statement to *sometimes* later on. When a sentence opens with *Unfortunately, however,* one word is redundant; but when a sentence opens *In addition, however,* do the road signs mean go ahead or turn around? And what can a *substantial vacuum* possibly be, or not be? Statuary might include human figures in concrete, but it is difficult to picture a *concrete human being.* Nor can persons be *held in low esteem* and things be *used to poor advantage.* On coming across such incongruities, a reader can only surmise that the writer's thinking may be less than admirable. Yet these samples are quoted from actual business writing.

The words *generally* and *usually* are inserted for the purpose of hedging statements. When there is no cause for hedging, these words are best omitted. More seriously, to build up an unnecessary *generally* into *as a general rule* is unforgivable. Sometimes a general rule is properly invoked along with, or in contrast to, special rules, but the phrase *as a general rule* should never be made to substitute for *generally*—assuming the latter word is itself appropriate. Finally, the word *normally* should not be used as a mere substitute for *usually*, because *normality* carries a suggestion of conformity to a standard.

Casually adding *etc.* or *and so on* to a series does nothing for the reader. The words may suggest that the writer would have added more items but for time constraints or laziness; nevertheless, the impression left by *and so on* ranges from vagueness to puffing, except in those instances where the rest of the series has been given before or it is obvious—as in *A,B,C, and so on.*

◇ Fourth, the articles *the, a* and *an* should be looked at a second time whenever they appear. It is surprising how many business writers slow down their readers with burdensome excesses of *the*. The remedy is to reread each sentence and examine every *the*. If a phrase sounds right without *the*, remove it. If not, then try substituting *a* or *an*. Now if the substitute works better than the original *the*, let *a* or *an* stand. Seldom does the reverse process—replacing *a* with *the*—result in a gain. Nevertheless, such tests should also be made, just to be sure.

◇ Fifth, excessive use of nouns gives the text a pompous sound. To achieve a bright, lively style, avoid nouny writing by putting verbs to work, letting them carry as much of the meaning as possible. *Recognizing superiority* is better than *in recognition of superiority; obeying a law* is preferable to doing things *in obedience to the law;* to *create* is better than to *perform an act of creation.* Stock phrases in particular should be scrutinized for possible replacement: to *communicate with by mail* is to *write to.*

Another type of nouny writing strings out nouns as modifiers. As an extreme case, consider what the sequence *materials inventory management report preparation* does to a reader as he adapts from one concept to another before finally realizing that the subject is *preparation*—not *report,* not *management,* not *inventory,* not *materials,* but *preparation*—the term that appears last. Noun modifiers as such are acceptable, even necessary; But they're not pearls to be strung out and hung around the reader's neck. He may be reminded of an albatross, instead. Three nouns in a row is a reasonable limit.

◇ Sixth, abstract writing generates an aura of vagueness. One symptom of abstract writing is excessive appearance of the suffix *-tion*, as in this example: *A survey laid the current difficulties to the imposition of mechanization on the former manual operation, whereas, instead, an entirely new system to fit in with the machine's capabilities should have been devised*. A business writer less addicted to the abstract might have said, *A survey disclosed the source of the trouble. Instead of devising new systems to employ the machine's capabilities, the firm had merely transferred its old system from manual to machine methods*. Nouns denoting concrete things are always preferable to abstract nouns. Also, a word like *conceptualization* is formed in several stages: *conceive, concept, conceptual, conceptualize, conceptualization*. Rightly used, there is a place for *conceptualization*, but the word must never be made to stand for *concept*. *Conceptualization* denotes a thought process, whereas a *concept* is the idea the process produces. *Limitation* is likewise distinguished from *limit: limitation* is the act of putting a *limit* on something. *There is a limit* (not *a limitation*) *on a taxpayer's deductions for contributions*.

Similar to abstract writing is subjective evaluation without factual support. To say that *the yield on a bond is high* conveys information, but adding the precise yield would convey more. Contrariwise, most people would find it difficult to assess the statement, *Average annual rainfall in New Mexico is eight inches*. Without a point of reference, *eight inches of rain* means little; a descriptive word would help in this case. Especially when writing for a heterogeneous audience, it is best to combine a descriptive word with a quantifier; for example, *Production for the week was a high 5,000 tons*.

Even descriptive words can be made more definite. Before calling an idea *interesting*, consider what creates that interest. Is the idea *unusual,* or *indicative of a trend,* or *profound?* Words should be selected for their ability to convey as much meaning as possible.

When verbosity is eliminated from business writing, readers can rejoice. It is tiresome to read that an activity *was experiencing difficulty* when, in simple terms, it *had trouble.* The person who says *We are incorporating into a coordinated operation separable and distinct activities, which go on independently from one another* can do his audience a favor by reducing his sentence to *We are coordinating activities that are independent.* Using the same words—but fewer of them—adds immeasurably to the impact of the sentence.

A word of caution is necessary here about how a simple, active verb can cause trouble, a situation that occurs frequently enough to warrant attention. Take the sentence, *The kind of customer a firm attracts affects its operations.* The juxtaposition of two active verbs, each with a different subject, is confusing enough to be avoided at all costs. Here *firm* is the subject of *attracts,* and *kind* is the subject of *affects.* Such a sentence must be rewritten. *A firm's operations are affected by the kind of customer it attracts* uses a passive verb to make an unambiguous statement. *The kind of customer a firm attracts will have an effect on its operations* is also better than the original, even though it employs a combination of verb and noun to replace a verb alone.

Despite what has been said, a lean style of writing still calls for development of each idea into a full paragraph. Audience direction still calls for the insertion of polite words and transitions as a courtesy. Readability still demands that a pleasant rhythm be maintained, even at the cost of inserting an extra word here and there. For above all else, rhythm is what makes prose readable; and the single greatest rhythm defect in business writing is a succession of accented syllables, as in *warehouse space use study.* Two accented syllables together are too many. Three (*space, use,* and *stud-*) are so cumbersome as to make the copy virtually unreadable. *Study of methods for improving the use of*

space in warehouses comes off much better, and it still qual-
ifies as lean writing.

The obvious test of rhythm is reading aloud. The words
should flow smoothly. Any sentence that causes tripping
over one's tongue mustn't be permitted to stand. In good
business prose, rhythm patterns are varied to avoid the
monotony of a marching beat or the mesmerizing effect of a
lullaby. The business writer who puts to use the innate
sense of rhythm he was born with is well on the way to a
readable style.

When the rhythm is offensive, four kinds of change are
available: deleting words, inserting words, switching
words, and changing words for the specific purpose of alter-
ing the rhythm pattern. Sometimes a sentence should be
broken up in the interests of a readable rhythm; subordinate
clauses are remade into whole sentences. All the methods
work; and smooth reading is worth the effort expended in
achieving it.

Inserting words to improve the rhythm of a sentence is a
delicate matter; if it is overdone, the business writer will
find himself bogged down again in the verbosity he had
rejected earlier. But there is considerable space for exper-
imentation in the spectrum between terseness and turgidity;
and if an excess of either style must be shunned, then a
certain amount of loosening must be welcome. Since the
goal is avoidance of both extremes, the watchword is
moderation.

Style and the reader

Beyond cultivating a lean, readable style, a business
writer can enhance his appeal to readers by the proper use
of variety, subtlety, personalization, and a light touch. From
the reader's standpoint, leanness saves time and readability
saves trouble. Leanness and readability might be described
as businesslike; and on the personal side, too, there are matters of style that can ensure acceptance of a piece of writing.

Business topics are often dull, and the messages

transmitted in business transactions, however necessary, can become tiresome. If, in addition, the writing style grows monotonous, the effect on readers must be deadening. To counter this threat, Harry Burns consciously dedicates himself to turning his back on the kind of writing he is most frequently exposed to. His use of variety, among other techniques, may never earn for his writing a prize for its vivid portrayal of life, but his material will at least become bearable.

As noted previously, variety can be introduced in many ways. Paragraphs can be developed by a succession of methods. Questions, exclamations, and verbless sentences can replace declaratory statements here and there. A passive verb can substitute for the active voice on occasion. Inversions can be designed to produce an extraordinary effect. A long sentence can be inserted among short ones, and vice versa. Even a negative construction can be used once in a while. As the writing shifts from one variety of statement to another, a richer, more interesting style is bound to evolve.

Nor is that the whole story. To make full use of variety, a writer must seize on its potential for gaining emphasis. Anything different is conspicuous. By calling attention to itself, a sentence that stands out from those around it lends emphasis to its message—and that emphasis should not be wasted on something routine. It's far more effective to use variety to emphasize points that deserve special treatment. A short sentence following a long one can carry a lot of punch. Try it and see. The object of an act, or the act itself, can be pointed to emphatically by a passive sentence. An occasional question can bring the audience up short. When not overdone, negatives can become a cogent device for emphasizing a point. The potential of all these variants from the standard affirmative, active, declarative sentence should not be wasted on trivia.

The use of variety to emphasize points has a subtle impact on readers. In addition, subtlety itself is a technique that can be employed in other ways to gain reader acceptance. Harry Burns is often confronted with heterogeneous audiences, representing diverse levels of knowledge of the subject at hand. How can one piece of writing explain basics to some readers in a way that won't lose them and at the same time hold the attention of more advanced readers long enough to get another message through to them? Harry's answer lies in subtly slipping fundamentals into the early discussion—perhaps as part of a review of what has been happening, or as a series of premises on which his conclusions rest, or as an attributive statement recognizing the contributions of others. Instead of saying *A is B and C is D* (you dumbbells), a subtle approach says in effect, *This will bring you up to date on what is going on. Recognizing that A is B and C is D, so-and-so went on to demonstrate.* . . . Subtlety takes many forms, all of them capable of flattering careful readers without offending knowledgeable ones.

A less subtle pitch for reader interest lies in personalization, mainly by use of the word *you*. Prohibitions against the pronouns *I* and *me* have been swept away; but *I* can never impress a reader as favorably as *you*. So talking about personalization means talking principally about *you* (the reader).

The pronoun *we* can breed ambiguity. It can signify reader and writer in concert, the writer and his associates, or the world at large. In addition, the editorial *we* means *I*. Inconsistency in use can compound the confusion. Obviously, *we* must be used with care.

Another way to personalize a piece of writing is by referring to people rather than abstractions. Polly Richardson does not talk about *supervision* in the abstract when she can be talking about a flesh-and-blood *supervisor*. Better still, she gives the supervisor a name, and *Ed Johnson* becomes someone readers can identify with. Thus, abstract writing can be avoided by *personalization* as well as by substituting concrete *things* for concepts.

Carrying the method in another direction, personification of inanimate objects invests them with an aura of excitement and drama. Computer people speak of *telling* their equipment to do things. Polly can also *instruct* machines, so long as precision is not sacrificed: it is often necessary to distinguish between *programming,* *feeding input,* and *modifying a control panel,* all ways of *instructing.*

A piece of writing must adopt a viewpoint. When the viewpoint she adopts comes from outside the subject, Polly will find herself writing in the passive voice: *data are fed to a computer and output is produced.* But if she adopts the computer's viewpoint—so that *it receives data and produces output*—she can avoid excessive reliance on the passive and restore an active character to her writing. Thinking in terms of a personified machine produces the desired change.

A changed viewpoint can lend vitality to writing in many situations. *A manager who neglects his assistants cannot be expected to earn their loyalty*—this changes to the active voice with a shift in viewpoint: *A manager who neglects his assistants cannot expect to earn their loyalty.* Likewise, a symptomatic viewpoint may produce more direct wording than a causative viewpoint. Instead of *In many cases, these errors are a result of faulty systems design,* the message can be put more directly: *These errors indicate faulty systems design.*

A few words of caution on the matter of viewpoint. Sudden switches in viewpoint, as from an objective view to the reader's perspective to the writer's vantage point, can bewilder a reader. At some point, Ed Johnson may become so disoriented by the switches that he abandons the effort to recover his bearings. Especially in short pieces of writing, consistency of viewpoint is a virtue, unless compelling reasons dictate a change.

In business communications, a personal, self-oriented viewpoint is dangerous for writers, and sometimes embarrassing to readers, because it proclaims a self-centered personality at work. Worse still is the self-conscious style that beginners sometimes fall into. *When I was asked to write about my project, I began to wonder what I ought to say*— that is no way to appeal to Ed Johnson. Why should he be interested in the writer's introspection? Ed is more concerned with his own problems.

Undoubtedly the most effective technique for ingratiating oneself with readers is to vivify one's style with touches of humor. In a world that is often bleak and grim, no one is so blessed as the person who can bring a warm ray of light and an invigorating moment of cheer into the lives of less fortunate associates. Gentle, inoffensive wit captures a willing audience. Dry, subtle humor enhances the effectiveness of a serious presentation to intelligent people. Laugh-provoking, good-natured fun provides a welcome relief from boredom for all of us. Opportunities to relieve the human condition with a touch of brightness should not be overlooked. Humor is the best antidote for boredom, and the most effective way to gain an edge over stolid competitors.

Polly looks for ways to inject an unusual turn of phrase, a novel juxtaposition of ideas or situations, an analogy that lightens a subject. In her experience, even puns aren't as objectionable as they're reputed to be. What does hurt attempts at humor, and causes them to fail, is staleness or straining. Novel touches that come easily stand a good chance of succeeding.

A further benefit is that a good-humored, courteous attitude forestalls bombast. The overblown language associated with pretentiousness stems from preoccupation with oneself and the impression one is making. In a word, audience direction—interpreted to mean concern for the readers—will preclude pompous writing.

In the end, style is essentially a matter of good taste. Our discussion of style began by offering specific advice on methodically cultivating a lean, rhythmic style for improved readability. That was followed by a section adding practical suggestions for increased acceptability among readers. The good taste that supplements these techniques may be acquired by reading with discernment and by learning to predict the reactions of the people one deals with. For taste, too, must be audience-directed. What is calmly accepted by some readers may be anathema to others, and a business writing style ought not to offend any group.

Literary allusions are like fire. Kept under control, they can be useful, but allowed to go unchecked, they are dangerous. Be sure your readers are familiar with an allusion, or else explain it fully and subtly when you use it. Even then, limit the number of allusions you employ, and make sure they're apposite.

It all adds up to being human as well as correct. The trend toward informality in society has exerted its influence on business—stuffiness is out, relaxed attitudes are in. However, a folksy style is often out of place in business writing, and a breezy style risks being dismissed as flighty when the business writer in fact wants to be taken seriously. The honest, open style, on the other hand, is always well received. In addition, punch is expected in the presentation of news and sales pitches, and a lean style is appreciated most in all presentations. To sum up, the business writer must keep his purpose in mind, direct everything toward accomplishing that purpose, and spell out his message in a straightforward, economical manner.

11 | *the building blocks*

Both written and oral communications are verbal; that is, they use words to convey meaning. Pictures may be added to illustrate certain points; gestures and facial expressions may help a speaker get an idea across; but the essential elements of speech and writing are words. Hence, the audience-directed approach requires that a writer select his words for optimal appeal to his audience. At the same time, preference should be given to words that work harder by carrying fuller meanings with greater precision.

Word selection

A high-level vocabulary will lose an uneducated audience, whereas low-level diction may offend an educated group. Talking down to people is no less risky than talking over their heads. Whatever the intellectual level of the readers, they should be addressed in words that are familiar to them. This is a far more appropriate criterion for selecting words than their mere length. *Undomesticated* is recognizable to many more readers than *feral; ergo* is more likely to be considered pretentious than *therefore,* a longer word. Once more, the short-short-short shibboleth doesn't address the real problem. It didn't work for paragraphs; it didn't work for sentences; and it doesn't work for words, either. Familiarity is a more reliable guide.

To find the language his associates and other audiences are acquainted with, Harry Burns listens to the words they use in speaking and observes the vocabulary they're exposed to in their regular reading. Similar projects should be undertaken routinely by business writers as part of their indoctrination in audience direction.

This method cannot, of course, resolve all doubts: questions will remain. A colleague is surprised to learn that oscillations are *damped* when they are reduced in amplitude; another tells you that *cull* is an unusual word; should Harry Burns drop these words from his vocabulary? A reasonable answer is to allow a certain number of risky words, neither so rare as to startle nor so common as to be part of every educated vocabulary. Also, some words that are indeed unusual have no satisfactory replacement. The golden mean is an adequate rule: Neither expunge such words nor overdo their employment. In writing for most of the audience, one need not pander to every last reader who may happen along.

Regardless of its length or familiarity, every word must of course carry the precise meaning intended. Only after two words have passed the test of precision should the more familiar of them be selected. In this selection process, precision is not impaired by a trade-off with readability; such a trade-off applies only to elaboration and detail. No matter how extensive one's vocabulary, the precise word is always the correct word. That rule holds for letters and memoranda as well as for procedure manuals and directives.

To satisfy his own objectives as a business writer, Harry Burns finds it necessary to develop a vocabulary adequate to provide precise words as they are needed. (The process requires a continuing effort on his part.) In addition, all business writers must respect distinctions between synonyms. Those who find themselves repeatedly *determining* things would do well to look into the exact meanings of *discover, ascertain, confirm, verify, corroborate, decide, settle,* and *resolve.* Likewise, for improved expression, it is useful to investigate the differences between *disclose, divulge,* and *reveal;* and between *inform, notify, apprise, tell, acquaint, familiarize,* and *communicate.* No special significance attaches to these examples: large numbers of synonyms are employed by business writers, and there is much ground to cover. However, the study of synonyms need not become a high-pressure project. For Harry, reflecting at leisure on the distinctions within groups of synonyms has been entertaining as well as instructive. For others as well, this specialized pursuit of common words and their meanings will bring greatest enjoyment as a spare-time hobby undertaken at a leisurely pace.

In part, the fine distinctions between synonyms are based on the connotations associated with words having like denotations. Business writers cannot afford to ignore such connotations, because they become part of the message a reader will receive. For example, frequent use of a word in a certain context can color its meaning for groups of readers. A statistician may have to describe a *bias* in data, but he should recognize that many of his readers will view the term as having more to do with sociological factors or social injustice than with sampling techniques. Nontechnical use of such a word should be avoided. Similarly, since *integrate* may arouse emotional responses, it is better at the present time to *consolidate* functions, *merge* operations, *combine* forms, and *integrate* racial groups.

Time spent in developing an extensive vocabulary and in learning the distinctions between words is well spent. However, a large vocabulary must not be perverted or abused. Its purpose is to provide a business writer with a means for achieving precision. Merely showing off one's acquaintanceship with large or unusual words is not a legitimate aim. Moreover, the careless misuse of words becomes more ludicrous as the words grow longer and more pretentious. And reckless use of synonyms merely to avoid repetition of a proper word is a mistake to be avoided. When *ambulating the canine* becomes part of everyday speech (heaven forbid!), we can all feel safe in talking that way. Meanwhile, let's *walk the dog*–instead of putting on the dog.

Insidious problems

Some writing problems can be avoided only by paying special attention to them. Figures of speech carry literal meanings that cannot be safely ignored. One may describe a communications problem as a *barrier to be surmounted or cut through*, but if a writer chooses to refer to the problem as a *gap*, then he can no longer *surmount* or *cut through:* the *gap* will have to be *bridged*. Simple as this rule appears, it is violated repeatedly in business writing, out of obvious carelessness. Mixing metaphors—changing horses in midstream—betrays similar carelessness. As an example, *grist for the trained eye* leaves considerable doubt as to the author's intent. A business writer may use a series of metaphors to make a point, but he must not create a monster by combining incompatible images. Among incongruities, *broad depth* is incomprehensible. A reader is entitled to infer that such recklessness of expression bespeaks carelessness in thinking, insufficient attention to detail, and discourtesy to the audience. Among borderline cases, *far nearer* and *grow smaller* may not disturb many people, but careful readers will wince occasionally.

Foreign phrases often create needless difficulty for readers. The literal meaning of *vis-à-vis* is *face-to-face*. To write *vis-à-vis* for *as compared with* is to use a metaphor involving foreign words, a practice not to be recommended. In speaking, the French *au fait* (to the point), when it is not mistaken for the slang *ofay*, is likely to engender uneasiness, because most listeners will have no handle with which to extract a meaning. However, *de novo* can be understood by people who have not seen it before, and it has a precise meaning not easily expressed in English: *anew* and *afresh* sound pedantic, and *all over again* and *from scratch* are not quite the same. Similarly, *quid pro quo* (literally, *this for that*), is often preferable to *something in exchange*.

Rhyming words and echoes have a habit of stealing unnoticed into prose and disconcerting careful readers. The only known protection is to reread copy for the specific purpose of discovering unwanted rhymes, echoes, or alliteration. There is no excuse, of course, for anything as obvious as this literary monstrosity: *Sales volumes attained contained stock market influences.* . . .

No matter how familiar you may think an acronym or abbreviation is, it could trouble some readers. For that reason, the first time an acronym or abbreviation is used, it should be explained, either parenthetically or indirectly, by spelling out the full title. Even as widely known an agency as the FDA should be called the Food and Drug Administration the first time it is named in a piece of business writing.

Jargon and pomposity

In every field, specialists develop words that thereafter are understood only among initiates. The underlying motivation for such technical jargon ranges from justifiable to mischievous. There may be an understandable desire to simplify communication by giving a name to something in order to avoid endlessly describing it. Even more defensible is to recognize a need for a term more precise than those already in existence. Experts do need new words to describe their discoveries and inventions. Imprecise language and endless repetition of descriptive passages can be avoided by using a neologism that is either a freshly coined word or an old word given a new, technical meaning. However, much jargon appears to have no better reason for being than to baffle outsiders and create a spurious air of sophistication among an ingroup. Regardless of origin or motivation, *buzz words* are seized upon and spread by so many people that conscientious business writers will have difficulty deciding whether to use or avoid them.

Those legitimate neologisms that improve communication should be used, but only after being defined so that readers understand their precise meaning. Definitions may be presented either subtly or directly with equal effect. However, illegitimate buzz words thrown about by supercilious persons to establish a presumption of knowledgeability or superiority should be handled cautiously. Writing that is meant to endure should adopt recent coinages slowly, and then only if they show signs of longevity; and they should of course be dropped quickly when they appear to be going out of style. More leeway can be permitted in casual speech, provided there is no risk of confounding listeners, and the particular word or phrase has not been overworked.

When a common word is given a new, technical meaning, the danger of misunderstanding is greater than when a new word is coined. Sometimes different disciplines latch on to the same word, each imparting its own meaning and contributing thereby to the general confusion. For example, a mathematician's *game strategy* applies to all situations in which participants exercise options that affect the probabilities of success of other participants; but a psychologist who talks of *games* is thinking solely of insidious strategems. Strategies versus stratagems, with a world of difference between them. Furthermore, to computer people, *games* are exercises in simulation, based on mathematical models that reflect the essential relations and parameters of the real world. Clearly, a lay reader, stumbling over the word *game,* needs guidance as to the particular meaning intended.

Much of what is known as *bureaucratese* or *gobbledygook* is not really jargon, but rather an overblown manner of writing. Far too many business writers reach for long words, *endeavoring to secure maximum utilization of existing equipment* when they should be *trying to use the machines they have.* There is no excuse for such pomposity.

It is in fact laughable: perhaps nothing more need be said about overblown language. The additional fact that it is widely employed in misguided efforts to display erudition is saddening. There are easier ways to appear ridiculous.

Misused words

Business and technical writers have developed a body of misused words that neither qualify as jargon nor serve any useful purpose. They are plainly mistakes that have been thoughtlessly perpetuated and that ought to be corrected in the interests of clarity.

One such abused word is *parameter*, which seems to have been corrupted by its similarity—in sound only—to *perimeter*. A *parameter* is neither a boundary nor a limit nor an option nor an ordinary variable (in the algebraic sense). It is a value that remains constant within a given system while varying from one system to another. Thus, gravity is virtually constant on earth, constant on the moon, but different as between earth and moon. So gravity is properly called a parameter. In common with all other parameters, it helps to define a system—in the case of gravity, a system of forces on earth, on the moon, or anywhere else.

Another frequently misused word is *reticence*, which many people seem to confuse with *reluctance*. Actually, *reticence* refers to one kind of reluctance only: an *unwillingness to speak*. Hence, it is incorrect to talk of a *reticence to act*.

Operative is mistakenly used as a synonym for *operating*. When a causal factor is at work producing an effect, for good or ill, that factor is *operative*. Thus, quality control may be *operative* in correcting the faults of an *operating* plant. A system is *operational* when it has been installed, tested, and found capable of functioning. Thus, a standby system may be *operational*, but not *operating* at a given time.

Definitive is often used as though it were a mere synonym for *definite*. A *definite* statement is straightforward, leaving no room for doubt as to where one stands. A *definitive* statement carries the weight of authority in resolving an issue. Also, a problem is *defined* when it is analyzed and described.

There is a clear distinction between *disinterested* and *uninterested*. A *disinterested* party has no stake in the outcome, whereas an *uninterested* party doesn't give a damn.

Since *sheer* means *alone,* to write *sheer size, scope, and complexity* is meaningless. *Sheer size* says *size and nothing else.* But what can *sheer size, scope, and complexity* possibly mean? Yet this type of solecism is encountered frequently in business writing.

The root word for *cordial* means *heart.* Hence a *cordial* welcome or a *cordial* relation is *warm, sincere, heartfelt.* It most certainly is not *superficially pleasant.*

Spasmodic, derived from *spasm,* is an ugly word denoting *convulsive* activity. *Irregular occurrence* is better described as *sporadic;* and *recurrent* phenomena may be *intermittent. Continuous* means without a break. Intermittent action that recurs over a long period may be called *continual,* but not *continuous.*

A thing can be *relatively* new, *relatively* expensive, or *relatively* harmful only with respect to something else. The notion of an absolute relativity is a contradiction in terms. Hence the word *relative* should be confined to situations where comparisons are being made.

A *bimonthly* report is issued once in two months, whereas a *semimonthly* report comes out twice a month.

A statement may *imply* more than it says, but it is the listener who *infers* hidden meanings. The words *imply* and *infer* are not interchangeable.

A person may be *delegated* to represent another, or he may have authority *delegated* to him. On the other hand, a person may be *relegated* to an inferior position, or to oblivion.

An amendment may *substitute for* original wording, in which case the original wording is *replaced by* the amendment; but the original wording cannot be *substituted with* the proposed amendment, as business authors have written. Furthermore, the amendment is an *alternative*, not an *alternate*. To *alternate* is to go back and forth; and a group that meets on *alternate* Tuesdays will be meeting every other week.

Some technical words and combinations of words are bandied about by business writers in disregard of original meanings. Thus, *significant difference* loses some of its precision when used loosely by nonstatisticians; and *discrete* is unfamiliar as a substitute for *separate* or *discontinuous*. A *leading indicator* is not a prominent pointer, but rather a harbinger—a measure whose variations foretell what another variable will do. Such an indicator *leads*, whereas other measures *lag*.

To *quantify* is not merely to *count* or to *number:* it is also to *measure* or to *express a quantity*. The word is useful in describing activities in which a system of measurement is imposed for the purpose of comparing or grading specimens. Thus, levels of air pollution may be *quantified* by measuring the density of airborne particles (as in a pollen count) or by testing for toxicity among humans. The temperature-humidity index is another example of *quantification*. Incidentally, *quantize* is entirely out of place in business writing. The term comes from quantum physics, and its meaning there is technical.

It is hard to understand how such an outlandish construction as *imbalanced* could appear in reputable publications; yet it does. Perhaps it is like whistling into the wind to suggest that the participial form of the verb *unbalance* is *unbalanced*. Of course, typists transcribing from pencil copy have a difficult time distinguishing between *un-* and *im-*. Nevertheless, *imbalanced* must be resisted as an impossible derivation from a noun whose parentage is itself doubtful.

Another word that ought to be avoided is *demean*. Since it has two distinct denotations, a neutral one relating to *demeanor* and a pejorative one relating to *mean* (in the sense of *base*), the word *demean* is ambiguous. By contrast, *be-*

mean has but one denotation that it carries unmistakably: to *debase*. Consequently, *bemean* is preferable for its clarity.

With such words to draw on as *start, begin, initiate,* and *commence,* it is an act of cruelty to perpetuate so unfortunate a neologism as *initialize,* which could easily be mistaken for an act of affixing one's initials to a document.

To *comprise* is to *include*. Those who write that a *division is comprised of four departments* are confusing *comprise* with *compose*. That division *comprises* four departments.

Utilization is not a fancy substitute for the noun *use,* just as *utilize* is not a substitute for the verb *use*. To *utilize* is to *adapt to a use not originally intended*. In an emergency, a paper clip may be reshaped and *utilized* as a collar stay, while similar clips are regularly *used* to hold papers together. However, a second definition of *utilization* in business relies on a long-established meaning: to *put to good use*. Thus, *utilization of resources* means *proper economical use,* as against a possibly wasteful or inefficient *using up* of materials, equipment, or labor. Also, a machine operating at 30 percent of capacity may be properly *used,* if it is making the product for which it was intended, but poorly *utilized,* because it is operating far below capacity. Further, another machine, working full time on the product for which it was intended, can also be *used* properly, and still be *underutilized,* in an economic sense, if it is capable of making a more profitable, or a more desirable, item.

The word *usage* refers to custom, but in business it has come to be regarded as a technical synonym for *consumption* (using up) in reference to inventories of materials. There is little likelihood that this neologism will spread beyond business terminology, so it should be employed cautiously, if at all, in addressing nonbusiness audiences.

To speak of *improving a problem* is careless. Situations are improved by solving problems, except in the special sense that an examination problem may be recast and thereby improved.

A *claim* asserts a *right*. There is no point in *claiming a loss,* except insofar as a tax refund or insurance reimbursement may be available.

A plant *burgeons* when it begins to grow. The word has a strong sound, reminiscent of *urge* and *surge;* and in figurative use, burgeon can accurately describe an *initial burst* or *breakthrough.* However, later growth, even though rapid, is not properly a *burgeoning.*

To *flaunt* is to display with ostentation; to *flout* is to treat with contempt. The two words are quite different.

A distinction should be observed between *rather than* and *instead of. Rather than* should be used only in those situations where a preference is intended.

Business writers apparently tire of ordinary words and look for elegant variants, with disastrous consequences. Here are some:—*Variegated* is sometimes found where *various* is intended. Unfortunately, *variegated* means *multicolored.* Those who are weary of *various*—as a great many writers ought to be—should try dropping the word without replacement. It usually contributes nothing to the sense. *To survey demographically institutions of variegated size and structure* probably meant little to the academic community that was being addressed, for institutional size and structure are not ordinarily perceived as being amenable to coloration.

⋄ *Discomfiture* is a matter of being completely undone. It is no substitute for the weaker *discomfort.*

⋄ A *truism* is not merely a *truth,* but an *obvious* truth that is hardly worth repeating.

⋄ *Fortuitous* means *accidental;* it does not mean *fortunate.*

⋄ *Taxable year* seems to be sanctioned by the Internal Revenue Code and Regulations. Nevertheless, *tax year* says it better.

Relationship is an overused word. The position of one individual, entity, or group with respect to another—of employer to employee, buyer to seller, political party to its candidate, affiliated companies to each other—is properly called a *relationship*. But individuals, entities, and groups may develop amicable *relations,* or disagreements may disturb *relations* between them. Clearly, *the relationship of a stockholder to a corporation* means something quite different from *the relations between the stockholder and the corporation*. However, the distinction between the two words is not always so clear. To cite a borderline case, *a cause-and-effect relation* is as appropriate as *a cause-and-effect relationship*. Here the advantage of *relation* over *relationship* lies only in its simplicity.

Recognition of a viewpoint, and adherence to it, can avert serious confusion in the selection of words. For instance, one company's payment is another company's receipt. In writing about an accounts receivable activity, the receiving company's viewpoint should be maintained consistently. Its mail brings *receipts,* and any mention of *payments* will only confuse readers—although *remittances* and *remittance slips* may properly be referred to, because the neutrality of these terms is well established in business usage. Similarly, *sales to customers* is an unambiguous, if redundant, phrase; but an expression like *customer purchases* can hardly be clear, except perhaps to the customer.

Euphemisms are not misused words; they are abused substitute words. Employing a euphemism to soften the harshness of reality, while perhaps a noble intention, is a futile gesture; for no matter how delicate a surrogate word may be, sooner or later it acquires the meaning of the word it replaced. Thus, to *let a person go* is to *fire him; termination* and *severance* are virtually synonymous with *dismissal;* and *separation* is almost as grim. Since euphemisms are transparent, the effort to invent new ones is singularly unrewarding.

Dysphemism—the use of an indelicate surrogate word—is much harder to account for than euphemism. Perhaps the leading business dysphemism occurs with the word *attrition,* which means to *wear down by friction*. That standard definition seems far removed from the thoughts of those who proudly assert that *staff reductions will be accomplished by attrition,* but some dictionaries list this as an acceptable usage.

Bordering on dysphemism is the use of *enormity* where *immensity* is meant. The *enormity* of a crime correctly refers to its exceptional wickedness and not its size.

The following sentence illustrates an indefensible combination of words frequently found in business writing: *Poor motivation cannot help but produce absenteeism.* Since either *cannot help producing* or *cannot but produce* would work, there must be an extra word in the original. *Can only produce* avoids the double-negative construction.

Other combinations involving negatives can be troublesome in business writing. In the following example, if *not less than* is replaced by *at least,* the meaning is retained and the reader's thought process is assisted: *Capacity was not less than 50 percent in excess of demand. In excess of* can also be replaced by *higher than: Capacity was at least 50 percent higher than demand.* Similarly, *not unlike,* an example of litotes, does little for a business writer. The way to achieve an appearance of moderation is to avoid overstatement. Artificial devices tend to annoy busy readers by their hint of pedantry.

A midcentury plague gives indications of subsiding, but unfortunate vestiges are still with us. There was a sort of game in which participants seemed to vie with one another to find words on which to tack the suffix *-wise.* Only *temperaturewise* could something be hot or cold. Instead of bad weather, there were bad days, *weatherwise.* One figure was higher than another *percentagewise.* An activity preceded another *timewise.* Having rediscovered such legitimate words as *lengthwise* and *likewise,* the founders of the game apparently dreamed of the day when every sentence would end in *-wise.* But the game attracts fewer devotees these days. It seems to be on the wane popularitywise, which is all to the good wisdomwise (or wisewise?).

Misspellings

Some words are so frequently misspelled that they deserve special attention. The most serious spelling errors, of course, are those that lead to confusion between words.

To illustrate, to *forgo* is to *pass up*, and an opportunity *forgone* is one that has not been seized. However, a *foregone* conclusion is one that was settled in advance; and *foregoing comments* refers to *previous comments*. The prefix *fore-*, which appears in *forewarn* and *foretell*, is not to be confused with the prefix *for-*, which is illustrated by *forget* and *forbid*. They come from different sources.

A similar confusion involves the suffixes *-for* and *-fore*. When speaking of a development and the reasons *therefor*—a stilted construction, in any case—the absence of a final *e* distinguishes the word from the familiar connective *therefore*.

Effect and *affect* trouble many people. In business usage, only *effect* is a noun, as in *cause and effect*. The verb *effect* is closely tied to the noun; it means to *bring about a result*. The verb *affect* is less cogent, meaning only to *exert an influence*, which may be either strong or weak. *Temperature may affect a machine's operation,* whereas *air conditioning can effect a lowering of ambient temperatures and all that may imply.*

To *appraise* is to *evaluate;* to *apprise* is to *inform.* Additionally, *apprise* is often too formal to be used comfortably in place of *inform*.

Straitjacket refers to a constraining device few people are familiar with. Since the word conveys a notion of stricture rather than of rectitude, it has no *gh*.

Re-sort, meaning to sort again, should be hyphenated to avoid conflict with *resort* and its meanings.

Those who must use the word *nit-picking* ought to recognize its association with *nits,* and not with *knits*.

Other misspellings that change the meanings of words involve *principle* and *principal*. A *principle* is a *concept,* an *idea.* A *principal* may be a *person acting in his own behalf,* a *partner in a firm,* or a *leading figure.* A *principal cause* is a *chief cause.*

Discrete, meaning *separable* or *discontinuous,* has been mentioned before. Those who are still enchanted by the word ought at least to keep it from corrupting *discreet,* meaning *judicious.*

For frequency of incorrect spelling, *incidentally* ranks among the leaders. Other misspelled words encountered in business writing include *occurrence, relevant,* and *accommodation.*

Uncertainties concerning the singular and plural forms of nouns cause spelling errors. The singular of *criteria* is *criterion;* the singular of *phenomena* is *phenomenon;* the singular of *data* is *datum;* the singular of *media* is *medium;* but *agenda* is accepted as a singular. Some Latin plurals are well established in English—*memoranda* is perhaps more familiar than *memorandums*—but other Latin plurals are less well entrenched: *formulae* is readily replaced by *formulas.* When in doubt, Anglicize, usually by adding an *s.*

Desirable has no *e* before *-able. Usable* is better without the *e;* but those who want their *e* may have it, and they will write *useable. Knowledgeable* takes an *e* after *dg,* whereas *judgment* is preferred over *judgement* (despite President Ford's trisyllabic pronunciation of the word).

Recision and *rescission* have similar meanings. Either one may describe a withdrawal of a previous pronouncement. But the words come from different roots; and hybrid spellings won't work.

Fun with words

The richness of the English language, owing to the diversity of its sources, provides unparalleled opportunities for precise expression. When synonyms are derived from two or more languages, a process of differentiation works to create useful distinctions, which a careful business writer may then employ advantageously.

A secondary benefit derivable from the nature of the English language and its history is the fascination awaiting those who pursue words to their sources. The pastime is also useful, in that it offers to expand one's insight into the language. That tracking down the origins of words can be fun is illustrated by the following words in common use:

⋄ The origin of *exorbitant* is quite clear: out of orbit, off the track.

⋄ *Affluence* flows toward, *effluent* flows away, *influence* flows inward, and *superfluity* overflows.

⋄ To *espouse* a principle is to *marry* it, naturally.

⋄ To *tax* is related to a root meaning to *touch*.

⋄ The original *symposium* was a *drinking party* (from *sym* or *sum*, together, plus *posis*, drinking).

⋄ To *connive at* is still to *close one's eyes* to wrongdoing (the original meaning); whereas to *connive with* now involves complicity.

⋄ *Manufacture* traces back to *make by hand*.

⋄ *Sophistication*, a word derived from *Sophist*, has always carried adulteration as one of its meanings.

⋄ From a single root meaning *measure* come such diverse words as *mode, model, moderate, module, modest, modify, mold, commodity*, and *accommodation*.

⋄ *Lax, relax, lease,* and *release* are related through a common ancestor originally meaning *loosen* and later meaning *allow*.

⋄ *Warranty* and *guaranty* come from the same root and are related to *warn, garnish,* and *garrison*.

⋄ To *garble* is to *sift;* hence, to give a one-sided account— and a *garbled message* is *one-sided*. However, another word for *sift* is the root for *crisis* and *criticism;* and the Greek word for *acting in a play*, derived from the same root, brings us *hypocrisy*.

⋄ A *crucial* point (from *crux*, a cross) is like a *crossing* in the road.

⋄ *Forlorn hope* comes from the Dutch *verloren hoop*—lost band—a suicide squad.

◇ One meaning of *addle* is *liquid manure*, a derivation that adds zest to the terms *addlebrained* and *addlepate*.

◇ Finally, *sesquipedalian*, an uncommon word, whimsically describes an addiction to long words by measuring them and finding their length to be *a foot and a half*, literally (from *sesqui*, one and a half, plus *ped*, foot).

12 | the last time around

Given the time pressures in business—and they are often inescapable—editing must be done quickly and efficiently. The first decision in reviewing a manuscript concerns the report's value. Considering the subject, message, and circumstances, how much reviewing and revising can be justified? How much time and effort should be expended, in light of what the report seeks to accomplish?

Next comes the review process itself. In conducting a review economically, checklists can help. The first list below is for both editing one's own business writing and reviewing the work of subordinates and others.

Checklists for business reviewers

SUPERFLUOUS WORDS AND PHRASES

⬦ For a lean style, delete every unnecessary word. Remember, however, that some words are necessary to pro-

151

mote readability. Look for familiar—and meaningless—expressions gratuitously thrown in.

◇ If two words mean nearly the same thing, the less expressive one must go. It doesn't help to describe something as *complicated and confusing*. Although there is a difference in meaning between the two words, one or the other (depending on the situation) will carry the intended thought well enough.

◇ Intensives can be justified only in rare instances. *Extremely* should almost never be used; and *extraordinary* should be reserved for instances that truly are far removed from the ordinary.

◇ Examine each word combination for possible replacement by a single precise word.

◇ Try a series of quick tests designed to eliminate superfluous words. Mentally delete the following words when you come across them, and strike out those that make no contribution to sense or readability: *the, an, a; that, which, who;* modifiers; clauses like *it should be noted that.*

Meanings

◇ Scrutinize words to be sure they carry the intended meaning.

◇ Ask whether other words would be more precise. Consider the connotations of synonyms, and select the most appropriate replacement words.

Sentence structure

◇ All sentences should be grammatically correct.

◇ Simplify unnecessarily complicated structures to make them easier to follow.

◇ Trace every relative pronoun back to its antecedent, to see that the two words are physically close and that they agree in number (both singular or both plural). If too much distance lies between a relative pronoun and its antecedent, restructure the sentence.

◇ A subject and its verb must agree in number. If subject and verb are so far removed as to make tracing difficult, then the sentence will undoubtedly gain from restructuring. Business writing should not pose a series of puzzles for readers to solve.

◇ Read each sentence aloud to ensure pleasing rhythm and readability. Also, listen for disconcerting echoes, rhymes, alliterations, or singsong passages.

AMBIGUITY

◇ Although most difficult to detect in one's own writing, ambiguity is often quite obvious to a reviewer. The sources of ambiguity are numerous. Look for words with multiple meanings, words that may be either nouns or verbs (with the same spelling), and dangling phrases attaching to the wrong words.

FAULTY PARAGRAPHS

◇ Every paragraph must have a topic sentence to pull it together.

◇ See that each paragraph develops one idea only.

◇ See that no ideas are left undeveloped.

◇ Ascertain that the development methods are compatible within a single paragraph.

Whereas the foregoing checklist serves a dual purpose—in editing either one's own writing or the writings of others—the following list is intended primarily for reviewing a draft someone else has submitted.

ALLOCATION OF SPACE

◇ Note how much space is dedicated to each subject, and

ask whether the proportions are reasonable. No minor matter should ever be treated at length simply because voluminous material is available.

LOGIC

◊ Follow the development of themes, asking whether it makes sense. The sequence should be defensible; there should be no gaps; and explanation of a concept should precede elaboration. In making these tests, it is often helpful to draw up an outline of your own.

◊ Take a second look at passages beginning with *therefore, hence, because,* and similar connectives; ascertain that there really is a logical connection.

◊ Scrutinize *buts* and *howevers;* replacement by *and* sometimes accords better with the facts.

COHERENCE

◊ Watch for abrupt shifts in subject or direction. Every section should have a transition sentence or paragraph.

◊ Provide readers with transitions between and within paragraphs to help them find their way.

AUDIENCE DIRECTION

◊ Since audience direction is the foundation on which good business writing rests, its application should be uppermost in a reviewer's mind. In fact, the reviewer's function is to represent the audience in suggesting changes to the author.

◊ The tone of writing should be courteous, or at least inoffensive. Contentiousness attracts notice for the wrong reasons. A soft tone is more likely to win adherents.

◊ The vocabulary should be suited to the readers. In reviewing a manuscript, scanning to gain an overall impression will generally suffice for evaluating the propriety of diction.

◇ Ambiguity that could lead to misinterpretation should be eliminated.

◇ Ask what the readers will come away with, and compare your answers with the benefits that ought to be derivable from a piece of writing on the same subject.

◇ Read and reread the manuscript through the eyes of the persons the author intends to reach, making the assumptions they're likely to make, and judging how they'll react and what they'll learn. Then answer the final question: *From the standpoint of the readers, is this manuscript worthwhile as it stands?* This epitome of audience direction is the key to successful business writing.

Relations with writers

An editor stands as a surrogate for the audience. Nevertheless, the editor of another's manuscript must accord certain considerations to the author.

First, an author has legitimate prerogatives. (Incidentally, the term *author* is used here to designate the person who signs a letter or memo, or whose name appears on a report or article. If a manuscript is ghostwritten, then the prerogatives described here belong to the author, as the person associated with the published piece, and not to the anonymous writer of the draft manuscript.) Questions of style, in particular, are for the author to decide; an editor should not presume to take such matters into his or her own hands. Personal preferences of authors must be respected whenever alternatives are available.

Second, diplomacy is important in editing, because of a sensitivity known as *pride of authorship*. Having created a manuscript, many persons are deeply offended by criticism of their efforts. They frequently resist all change—good or bad—and always on ostensible grounds having nothing to do with true motivations. An editor should ordinarily be content with *suggesting* changes, and should in no case feel free to go beyond *recommending* changes. Insistence is unlikely to succeed at the moment, and it may discourage later efforts.

Third, a properly handled review can be educational. The business reviewer should never lose sight of his potential for guiding a writer: it is most important, therefore, that the guiding hand be steady. Suggested changes must be defensible; and they must be contained within limits the individual writer can tolerate. In content and manner, criticism must be constructive.

In short, a business reviewer should offer sound, usable advice, scrupulously avoiding unnecessary changes, even though he might consider them desirable. He should not tamper with a writer's style, ego, or feelings. Any tendency toward purism on the part of a reviewer must be overcome. For purism in editing leads to stilted writing, offended writers, and editors out on a limb.

Authoritative sources

Manifestly, a business reviewer has to be ready to defend his position against an irate author. It is unwise to rely on an *ipse dixit* stance, posing as an oracle; or to risk a battle of wills leading to an impasse; or to "pull rank" on a subordinate. Therefore, reviewers of manuscripts should barricade themselves behind a number of reference works, which ought to be consulted on every doubtful issue before a confrontation develops.

Types of reference books are described here, rather than specific works.

Despite the quibbles of those who exaggerate the effects of subjectivity on individual reactions to words, and the claims of those who drastically overestimate the rate at which meanings of words change, the standard dictionaries —fortunately—accepted as authoritative. Hence, a busi- writer is justified in pointing to a dictionary definition ort his choice of a word. A business reviewer may ervations of one sort or another—the particular use may be frowned on by some authorities; another word may be more appealing; there may be a possibility of ambiguity—but if a dictionary definition confirms the writer's view, then let him have his word. Even if the writer has to turn to an unabridged dictionary to find his definition, he cannot be denied a word, unless his usage is listed as archaic, obsolete, vulgar, or slang.

However, if a dictionary compares several synonyms, explaining the fine distinctions between them, then the writer's attention may be called to these niceties, and he may be offered a chance to reconsider his choice. (Be prepared to hear him say, "I know you're right, but your word doesn't sound like *me!*") Furthermore, a dictionary of synonyms—dedicated entirely to fine distinctions and illustrative quotations—should be on an editor's desk for the enlightenment of writers, and for the editor's constant use, too.

Although many people use thesauruses, a dictionary of synonyms is far more helpful in searching for a word to convey a meaning precisely. Before buying a thesaurus, compare it with a dictionary of synonyms. You may change your mind.

Books on English or American usage are indispensable to an editor; he cannot have too many of them on hand. With very little duplication, these books offer fresh insights that impart a new comprehension of the language. Besides, they can be fashioned into clubs for beating recalcitrant skeptics into submission!

A manual of style is helpful in resolving questions concerning punctuation, capitalization, abbreviations, and customs relating to such matters as quotations, footnotes, and modes of address. Style manuals deal with questions of presentation, not with style of writing. Matters of writing style are treated in the books on usage.

Among the tables to be found in style manuals and dictionaries is a list of proofreaders' marks. In correcting copy and instructing typists or typesetters, much time can be saved, and many misunderstandings avoided, by adherence to these standard symbols. There is no valid reason to do otherwise.

The following list is a sampling of marks frequently employed in editing copy.

a̲̲	Capitalize (three strokes under a letter)
⫽	Change to lowercase (slash through letters)
⌄	Insert a comma
⊙	Insert a period
ⱽ	Insert an apostrophe
℘	Delete
⌣	Reduce space
⊂	Close up
∾	Transpose
¶	New paragraph indention
run in	No new paragraph
at⎮the	Separate words (line between them)
word̲	Italicize (underlining)

Miscellaneous reference sources include dictionaries and glossaries specializing in a variety of matters, including technical terms, abbreviations, word origins, and quotations. In addition, standard dictionaries include sections on language, style, etymology, usage, and related subjects.

Every serious business writer and reviewer must have immediately available at least one standard dictionary, a dictionary of synonyms, and books on standard usage. For many situations, specialized references will also be needed. To work with less than this minimum is to hobble oneself unnecessarily.

A word to the conscientious writer

When a serious writer submits his manuscript to a magazine, he hopes, among other things, to learn something from the changes the editor makes before publishing the piece.

For editing can serve as a form of criticism, and the suggestions of a competent editor can be profitably studied for the guidance they offer.

However, it's best to seek such guidance from galley proofs rather than page proofs or printed pages. Between the two proof stages stand certain strange practices indulged in by production editors. Consequently, writers must be forewarned of changes in their articles that can't possibly teach them anything. First, words may be added or deleted for esthetic reasons related to the space to be occupied and wholly unrelated to the meaning intended. This practice may be pursued column by column, adding here to lengthen one column while subtracting there to shorten another. Second, whole paragraphs may be removed merely to make the article fit the allotted space. Above all, a "widow"—a short line appearing at the top of a page or a column—must never be allowed to stand! So don't trouble yourself over changes that defy comprehension in writing terms. The best authors suffer these desecrations at the hands of the best editors. Sophisticated writers look the other way.

13 | *the business of speaking*

Other chapters have concentrated on content and text, whether communicated orally or in writing. This chapter continues the discussion of the spoken word on formal and informal occasions, comprising lectures, seminars, committee meetings, and conversations.

The spoken and the written word

The text of a speech published verbatim seldom matches the appeal of an article written specifically for readers; and an article read aloud is likely to be less successful than a speech prepared with listeners in mind. Audience direction must consider the activity an audience is engaged in: it must distinguish between reading audiences and listening audiences.

The risk of losing a listening audience is reduced when the presentation is easier to follow, and when it consciously tries to bring back those whose attention wanders momentarily. Accordingly, a speech—even on a formal occasion—uses a more familiar vocabulary, simpler sentences, and more repetition than an article or report on a similar subject would use.

All writing must avail itself of openings that define the subject and transitions that bridge the gaps between sections. In speaking more than in publishing, advantages can be gained by following the dictum, *Tell them what you're going to tell them. Tell it to them. Then tell them what you've told them.* This basic formula works well for speeches, and it can also be modified to improve transitions between major components: *Tell them where you've been and where you are now. Then tell them where you're heading.* Thus each transition becomes a milestone along the way.

In other words, regardless of the sequence in which it is outlined, the material for a speech can be worked into a basic structure of preparing the audience for what lies ahead, after reminding them of the ground that has been covered. Moreover, this review and preparation should come at regular intervals throughout a talk. The method of review and preparation is certainly audience-directed.

One more audience-directed characteristic of effective speeches remains: a friendly style and tone *in the writing.* To be sure, friendliness, courtesy, and a light touch are important in articles as well, but in speeches these qualities become an absolute requirement. Just thinking of a cold, rude, or heavy-handed talk emanating from a podium is enough to drive large numbers of listeners away!

Visual aids

Although a well-written speech is an essential beginning, it can be assisted by well-designed *visual aids*—or so it would seem. In practice, visuals and text must be coordinated so closely that they have to be prepared together.

Many speakers, loath to devote the time and expense that visuals demand, prefer to do without them. Nevertheless, these aids do accomplish several objectives for other speakers, who are willing to make them an important element in their presentations. Among the advantages derivable from visuals are these:

◇ By enlivening a presentation, visual aids can capture and hold the interest of an audience.

◇ By adding a visual dimension to an auditory one, visual aids permit an audience to perceive a message through two separate senses, thereby strengthening the learning process.

◇ By spelling out unfamiliar words; by presenting pictures, diagrams, or objects; and by portraying relations graphically, visual aids can help introduce material that is difficult or new.

◇ By remaining in view much longer than oral statements can hang in the air, visual aids can serve the same purpose as repetition in acquainting audiences with the unfamiliar and bringing back listeners who stray from the presentation.

Visual aids range from simple blackboard or sketch pad, for writing or drawing on, to projectors throwing color slides or opaque material on a screen. Techniques for preparing and arranging visual aids are beyond the scope of a book on business writing, but a few observations are in order concerning the interaction between these aids and a speaker's words.

Harry Burns likes to use visual aids, even though he has learned that they have a tendency to take over a presentation. To resist that tendency by superimposing visuals on a speech can be disastrous. Instead of helping, the visuals may detract from the spoken words by diverting the audience's attention. So Harry has learned to create his slides directly from his outline—with the help of an artist—and to build his text around them. In effect, he meshes the visual and auditory aspects of his presentation by talking about the slides or using them as springboards.

Harry has also learned that the quality of his presentation is judged in toto, with perhaps more weight given to the visual aids than to the text or delivery. In his best presentations, he threads the visuals, linking them by codes, color schemes, geometric patterns, and blowups of segments in order to gain coherence among the slides themselves.

Needless to say, he devotes much attention to slide concepts, draftsmanship, color, visibility, and impact—always with his audience in mind. Will the audience get the right message? Will they respect the quality of the presentation and react favorably? Will they see the relation between the talk and the slides? These are the questions that help him predict the effectiveness of a slide presentation.

Delivery

A business speaker's delivery can be helped by good writing. While delivery entails voice modulation, the reading is assisted in turn by rhythm written into the sentences. Good writing combined with good delivery will make a speech effective, whereas the absence of either ingredient can be disastrous. Just as monotonous delivery can destroy mellifluous prose, dull writing can mar the beauty of a well-modulated voice.

Harry Burns varies the pace of his delivery, speeding through the less important passages, slowing down to emphasize significant points, and pausing to let new material sink in. He finds it useful to remove long words from passages he intends to cover quickly. However, the presence of longer words in an essential passage helps him slow his delivery, thus emphasizing a point and contributing to the effectiveness of the presentation.

Harry also inserts an exclamation or short phrase here and there in his text to permit himself a sudden burst or a raised voice. Perhaps more speakers ought to resort to such a device to disturb the slumberers in their audience.

Incidentally, Harry marks his text, underlining the words he wants to stress, noting the places for short pauses and long pauses, marking inflections as rising or falling, indicating fast and slow passages, calling for loudness and softness. He borrows some symbols from sheet music, but any set of symbols familiar to a speaker, and used consistently, will do.

To further his efforts at achieving variety, Harry intersperses a touch of humor whenever possible to relieve the seriousness of business subjects. The drier a subject is, the more it can benefit from the lubricating effect of a witty remark. Here again, good writing can help a spoken delivery.

All business speakers who read from scripts will find it useful to try departing from the prepared text on occasion and interpolating passages extemporaneously. Surely some specifics are sufficiently familiar to any business speaker to embolden him to put aside his crutch now and then. The practice is useful; and more important, audiences respond well to such adventures. It is almost as though they recognize a courageous act and want to applaud it. After having deliberately wandered from her text on several occasions, Polly Richardson took to writing some parts of her talks in full while leaving other parts in outline form—a method well designed to introduce variety in her delivery without disturbing her peace of mind.

An important aspect of delivery is naturalness, to which simple language is a prerequisite. It is inconceivable that bombast could be enunciated in a natural manner; and pompous delivery can destroy a plainly written text. A confluence of natural writing and ease in speaking is essential to acceptance by a modern audience.

Speakers employ several devices for improving their delivery. The oldest technique is to watch oneself in a mirror; recording speeches and playing them back came later—and many speakers have been unpleasantly surprised by what they heard. Television equipment combines visual and audial aspects in an immediate replay that has helped many speakers to polish their delivery.

Since enunciation is an essential element of good speaking, and not everyone can safely assume his enunciation is up to standard, those who take their speaking seriously should concentrate on the process of producing correct sounds. Careful listening to good speakers will tell you what results to go after; speech experts can add advice on how it's done; and practice exercises will accomplish the rest. Before "going on" in front of an audience, try a last minute warm-up in the form of tongue and lip exercises: Touch each tooth separately with your tongue; alternately smile and purse your lips; make explosive "p" sounds.

Practicing some combinations of sounds helps. Try repeating aloud this mixture of old favorites and new tongue twisters—or make up your own:

◇ *The drawbridge dropped and the train started through.* (Slowly, concentrating on each sound in turn.)
◇ *A black bumblebee basked on a brown branch.* (Every "b" explosive.)
◇ *Bumper to bumper, the traffic backed up.*
◇ *Peter Piper picked a peck of pickled peppers; a peck of pickled peppers Peter Piper picked.*
◇ *How now, brown cow.* (Each *ow* is pronounced *ah-oo*.)
◇ *How do you do, Pooh-Bah.* (Get away from *duh* for *do* and *ya* for *you*, if that's one of your problems.)

Speaking informally

One of the serendipitous benefits that conscientious devotees of writing should derive is a heightened ability to speak informally, as panelists, committee members, or participants in seminars. In many ways, improved writing skills will augment one's ability to speak effectively.

First, adeptness in preparing outlines is essential to carrying listeners along. No matter how short a statement may be, it should have an introduction, a body, and a conclusion. It should also follow a logical sequence in making its points. And it will often benefit from the technique: *Tell them what you're going to tell them. Then tell it to them. Then tell them what you've told them.* In a word, every statement should be structured properly. As Polly Richardson discovered, familiarity with outlining methods for writing helps also to structure an informal talk in which the outline is constructed mentally and retained in the speaker's mind.

Second, in making each point orally, a business speaker can be more effective if she is experienced in developing paragraphs. The concept of developing each idea will serve a speaker well; the options for development will come to mind readily; the essential balance between generalizations and specific details will be maintained naturally; and rounded, complete paragraphs will enhance each statement's appeal.

Third, a business writer who habitually inserts transitions and connectives in her manuscripts will find that her oral statements are also more coherent. Audiences will follow more easily.

Fourth, not only is sentence structure improved by working over written sentences, but the facility so acquired is readily transferred to speaking. Although spoken sentences can be much looser, and a speaker has opportunities to clarify sentences by stressing the right words aloud, a knowledge of how to construct readable sentences is most useful to a business speaker on all occasions.

Fifth, vocabulary is similarly carried over to speaking, although it is inadvisable to struggle long and hard to find the precise words while speaking. Polly limits her spoken vocabulary to words that are familiar to her audience, and she settles for the words that occur to her quickly, rather than run the risk of sounding unnatural or uncertain because of a halting delivery. A business speaker has a second chance to get her meaning across by repeating a thought expressed in different language, and she can also rely on expression, gestures, tone of voice, and other aids unavailable to a writer.

Sixth, the audience-directed approach to business writing is exactly what a business speaker needs most for gaining and holding an audience's attention, getting her message across, and winning people over.

Seventh, those techniques that add up to a good business writing style are also helpful in gaining acceptance for one's ideas while speaking.

To sum up, there are many reasons why good business writing leads to good business speaking. Consequently, attention to writing skills is a good beginning for improved speaking.

Conversation

What has been said of informal business speaking extends to ordinary business conversations. Outlines, paragraph development, coherence, sentence structure, vocabulary, audience direction, and style are important elements of spoken as well as written messages. Hence familiarity with the basic principles of business writing improves one's conversational skills.

Perhaps all that remains to be said about conversation is that practice is essential to improvement, and that a person can practice on his own, without waiting for an audience to come along. Harry Burns's method is to select a subject in spare moments and say something about it—not always out loud, to be sure. The subjects may come from newspaper headlines, magazine contents, book or chapter titles, and overheard remarks. Once Harry has seized on a subject, he disciplines himself to pull his thoughts together and commence his statement within seconds, because promptness is one of the traits he wants to project. Sometimes he continues to develop a single subject until he runs out of material; at other times he sets a goal of talking two or three minutes.

Persons who talk too little do their associates a disservice. Failure to hold up one's end of a conversation is a breach of etiquette. Conversely, the person who recognizes a social obligation to participate in conversation, as in other activities, can enhance his standing among his associates by acquiring competence in self-expression through the suggestions offered above. A supply of topics and an ability to extemporize should be adequate to the demands of ordinary situations.

At another extreme, those who talk too much can benefit from a conscious effort to structure what they say. If they can learn to avoid rambling, stay with their subjects, make their points, limit their use of repetition, and bring their remarks to a suitable close, their acceptance among their associates will improve. Audience direction provides the key.

Disagreeing with others without offending them is largely a matter of stressing courtesy, which is itself audience-directed. Some people pretend to be playing devil's advocate, while others stress areas of agreement before moving on to subjects of disagreement. *Yes, but* . . . is generally more acceptable than *Well, no.* . . . Submerging one's beliefs is not necessary, provided that a sensitivity to others is retained. Nevertheless, in a business setting, debate is futile unless it influences a course of action. Challenging the chance remarks of others is a boorish practice, designed to win a reputation for contentiousness, and little else.

The place of dialog

To summarize, good writing provides a strong foundation for effective speaking. All the elements of business writing are useful to speakers in business; and that usefulness carries through formal, informal, and conversational speech. Audience direction is the underlying guide. Familiarity with the principles of business writing makes the methodology available. Practice does the rest.

Opportunities for self-expression abound. No one need sit silently by, failing, because of reticence, either to contribute to a dialog or to learn from the contributions others might have built on his own perceptions. Indeed, for those who aspire to leadership positions, few endowments are more valuable than articulateness. Anyone who learns to write well should not hestitate to transfer the acquired skills to speaking. Conversely, anyone who wants to speak well should concentrate on learning to write well. The two skills go hand in hand.

epilogue | *integrity courtesy enjoyment*

Good business writing involves mastery of many subjects, all of which have been covered in this book: words, sentences, paragraphs, structure, coherence, and style. Beyond such mastery are three important matters concerning the attitude of the business writer: integrity, courtesy, and enjoyment.

Above all else, the integrity of one's writing must be protected. An opening must offer a foretaste of the true subject, and not one that is presumed to be more popular. Gimmickry will only confuse, annoy, and repel readers. Alarming prognostications, extravagant claims, and overstatement of benefits arouse distrust that spreads to an entire report and its conclusions. Even minor misstatements of fact and "innocent" hyperbole are dangerous; meticulous concern for the authenticity of material is essential.

Ideally, a business writer should make every effort to understand his subject deeply. His research should penetrate to the core of each issue, and his explication should be forthright. Admittedly, time pressures and political consid-

erations often put the ideal beyond one's reach; nevertheless, whenever writing purports to reflect a logical relation
between events, there must be evidence of necessity and
sufficiency. Non sequiturs and patent superficiality destroy
reader confidence. Insights must be valid as well as fresh.

Clarity of expression is also related to integrity, for
vague, ambiguous, or confused statements leave the question of accuracy in doubt. Additionally, obfuscation and
ponderousness can only lead a reader to wonder, "If the
author really has something to say, then why doesn't he put
it in understandable language?"

Integrity has many aspects, all of which must be
guarded from flaws, lest the business writer's credibility be
called into question. Similarly, courtesy toward the audience must also manifest itself in many ways, to win readers
over, or at least to promote a favorable response to both the
business writer and his message.

It is courteous to deliver ideas instead of pouring out
mere verbiage. The pretentiousness of bombast can be
avoided by retaining respect for the intelligence of the audience, by paying attention to their needs, and by resolving
to help them. In addition, careful structuring relieves the
audience of an unnecessary burden in following an argument. An audience-directed approach is automatically
courteous.

Another aspect of courtesy surfaces in the process of
handling disagreements. It is better to try building a bridge
to one's opponents than to attack them. Unfair attacks are
anathema: the views of others must never be distorted, and
their motives must not be challenged. If the audience itself
is hostile, then tact is required to win it over. Arguments
should be presented in a positive light and made to stand on
their own; and always remember that your position is yours
to present, without apology. Above all, business writing
should always display good taste. The greatest courtesy a
business writer can show lies in making the effort to produce material of a high order of competence and readability.
Contrariwise, slovenly writing is an affront to the reader.

Finally, the business writer's mood is likely to show through his writing. Such lightness and warmth as dull subject matter will permit can be achieved only by a person who genuinely likes what he is doing. That observation should not be construed negatively; on the contrary, sharpened skills make writing easy, a knowledge of words and their origins adds enjoyment, and in the end a job well done provides gratification. So have fun, and let your readers know you're having fun. Let them enjoy it with you.

Although a piece of writing inevitably creates an impression on readers about the person who has written it, a business writer should not allow himself to indulge in self-conscious exhibitionism. Rather, he should let the audience's impressions derive from a straightforward, readable presentation characterized by tightness of organization, cogency of arguments, and precision in selecting words. And never forget that a lean, lucid style is the most appropriate one for a business writer to cultivate.

index